Turnbull Griffin Haesloop Architects

New York · Paris · London · Milan

Turnbull Griffin Haesloop Architects
Land and Light

Foreword by
Paul Goldberger

Contributions from
Daniel P. Gregory
Mary Griffin
Eric Haesloop
Donlyn Lyndon
Margaret Turnbull

6 **Foreword**
Paul Goldberger

12 **Preface**
Mary Griffin

16 **The Nature of Simplicity**
Daniel P. Gregory

22 Stinson Beach Oceanfront House
32 Sausalito Remodel
40 Connor Creek Ranch
50 Sea Ranch Bluff
60 Santa Lucia Preserve
72 Lake Tahoe Retreat
84 Sebastopol Camp
94 Grace Magill Arts and Science Building, Burke's School
98 Atherton Retreat

112 **Turnbull Griffin Haesloop Houses at The Sea Ranch**
Donlyn Lyndon

118 Sea Ranch Meadow I
124 Sea Ranch Meadow II
136 The Commons, Branson School
146 Douglas Fine Arts Center, Branson School
152 Hicks Mountain Ranch
162 Marin Hillside
174 College Track San Francisco
178 Sausalito Hillside Remodel
188 Coyote Camp
194 Hupomone Ranch
204 Cloverdale Vineyard
214 Berkeley Cottage
218 Sonoma Retreat
228 Stinson Beach Lagoon
238 Portola Valley Garden
254 Skyfall, The Sea Ranch
266 Carmel Valley Retreat
278 Healdsburg Knoll

292 **Paths**
296 **People**
297 **Chronology**
298 **Credits**
300 **Acknowledgments**
301 **Contributors**
302 **Photography**

Foreword Paul Goldberger

Legacy is a complicated business in architecture, as it is in any creative human endeavor, and even more so when an architecture firm is the continuation of a practice started by a revered designer who is no longer here. Turnbull Griffin Haesloop carries the name of William Turnbull, who rose to prominence in 1965 when, working with Charles Moore, Donlyn Lyndon, and Richard Whitaker, he designed The Sea Ranch Condominium 1 on the Pacific Coast in Northern California, a condominium project with simple, shedlike forms of wood and an environmentally sensitive site plan that made it one of the most influential projects of the era. The four formed a firm that would be short-lived: Moore, Lyndon, and Whitaker departed quickly to become the heads of three different architecture schools, leaving Turnbull to remain at his drafting board, practicing on his own in San Francisco and doing notable work that extended the sensitive and humane design stance for which all four partners had been known. In time he was joined by his wife, Mary Griffin, and by Eric Haesloop, both designers of originality and talent, and the firm expanded its scope. Turnbull died of cancer in 1997 at sixty-two, and since then Griffin and Haesloop have maintained the practice that he started, listing his name ahead of theirs in tribute to his role not only as founder, but as their mentor and design inspiration.

But Griffin and Haesloop have other things to say as well, designs that do not contradict the principles by which Turnbull designed but extend them and reinterpret them for a different time. This book is a record of their work over the nearly three decades since Turnbull's death, and it stands as a reminder that creativity must evolve constantly. The architecture of Turnbull Griffin Haesloop is not an attempt to make new versions of William Turnbull buildings, but to make new buildings that are consistent with his ideas and show that they can have meaning for different times and different places. That is one of the things that I mean when I talk about legacy being complicated: it involves the challenge of reinterpreting, of evolving, of making something that is your own even as you acknowledge the influence of a predecessor. It is a delicate balance between following and breaking away, and if you do it well, you can show that it is possible to honor the past and make something new at the same time, which is what Mary Griffin and Eric Haesloop and their colleagues at Turnbull Griffin Haesloop have done.

Their architecture has a crispness and a sharpness that you don't often see in Turnbull's work, which has something to do, surely, with the fact that we live in a more technologically driven age, and that even buildings that strive to be warm and humane may often have a technological edge to them. But Griffin and Haesloop's sharpness still bears the sensibility of Turnbull's softer, more comfort-driven aesthetic, which was always deeply connected to vernacular architecture. Turnbull, like Moore, Lyndon, and Whitaker, had the gift of being able to take elements of familiar and conventional buildings and make of them something that never seemed derivative, but instead fresh and original, and you can say the same thing about the work of his successors. Their houses, too, feel beautifully, almost magically, poised between the conventional and the special, between the familiar and the surprising.

The Sea Ranch Bluff, constructed on one of the few unbuilt oceanfront lots in the original section of The Sea Ranch development, makes the point. The elements that made the early Sea Ranch buildings iconic are still there: vertical wood sheathing, shed roofs. (Defying the modernist predilection for the flat roof was one of the things that made the original Sea Ranch so striking.) But now, more than a generation later, the facade is interrupted by a vast expanse of glass, broken into well-proportioned vertical panels and turning a corner to embrace the main living space. The details are more defined, the aura more precise. The new pays homage to the old and breaks away at the same time.

You could say the same thing about Meadow II, another house at The Sea Ranch that the firm added recently, in this case as a new main house for a family compound, the first portion of which the firm had designed fifteen years previously. The newer project is crisper, and has more glass, and the angled shed roof is long and gently hints at monumentality in its scale, but the wood and the carefully composed massing keep everything warmly comfortable.

Familiar forms provide the starting point for every one of these projects, either the forms of the surrounding context or the primal building shapes we all carry in our heads—or, as in the case of Sebastopol Camp, a house in Sonoma County, images of midcentury modernism, which here are reimagined with a kind of gentle verve. This is one of my favorite houses, not least because it meets you quietly, with a discreet facade, and then bursts open into a splendid wall of glass facing the forest. There are similar allusions to midcentury modernism in the Atherton Retreat, the Sonoma Retreat, and Stinson Beach Lagoon, all handled with equal aplomb. I don't think any of these houses is something Turnbull would have designed; he probably would have found midcentury modernism a bit too close to his own time for comfort, perhaps even a bit too Palm Springs-y. But Griffin and Haesloop have reinterpreted this style with self-assurance and ease, weaving it gracefully into the Turnbull legacy.

Their work is not limited to houses. Among the most pleasing of the projects here are the two buildings for the Branson School in Marin County, which raise to civic scale the same ideas that Griffin and Haesloop explore in the houses, and the Cloverdale Vineyard, where the industrial vernacular is made soft and inviting, yet never cute. These projects, like every piece of architecture presented in this book, emerge out of respect for what is there, for the architecture that has come before, and for the community of which it is a part—for the things these architects have inherited from the world around them, and which they use as the inspiration to make something fresh and new.

Preface

Mary Griffin

Turnbull Griffin Haesloop Architects: Land and Light shares twenty-seven projects designed by TGH over the past twenty-seven years. In this monograph, Eric Haesloop and I document the chapter we began after the death of William Turnbull Jr. in 1997. Both of us worked with Bill for over a decade and were deeply influenced by his design talent and values. We named our new practice Turnbull Griffin Haesloop, bringing our shared and collective experiences forward as we addressed a changing world. The design and construction of these projects involved many talented collaborators from both within and outside of the office including especially our partner Stefan Hastrup and interior designer Margaret Turnbull. Eric and I greatly appreciate the abilities and friendship of the talented people who contributed their expertise to our buildings. Finally, we are profoundly grateful for the trust, insight, and participation of our clients.

When working on the design of these projects certain values guided our process yet each project was unique. We listened to the site. As Eric often said, the land talks back to us. What were the essential qualities of the site? We looked at the arc of the sun, the slope of the land, the trees, and the views. We mapped the less visible concerns such as fault lines and poor soils. On more urban sites we considered the neighbors. What were the opportunities and constraints? How could our building frame or reveal the special qualities of the site?

We also listened to the owners. What was unique about how they wanted to live? What was their budget? How could our design enhance their lives and their experience of their site?

　A continued source for inspiration was precedent from both our Turnbull lineage and a rich tapestry of architectural and landscape examples. Increasingly we explored environmental considerations. What specific sustainable responses were appropriate for each project? Which new technologies could we explore? Designing many of our buildings on the Northern California coast has challenged us to create sustainable structures built to last in the face of severe threats such as fire, flooding, earthquakes, and landslides.

　All these factors fed into an iterative design process. Eric and I shared a table for designing. We sat across from each other and explored site and plan diagrams on tracing paper. Roof shapes were tested with cardboard models cut into contour bases. In more recent years, we increasingly modeled options on the computer. As the design direction developed, we frequently shared our progress with the clients, incorporating their suggestions. Once the overall diagram was set, we used detailing and materials to support the essential idea of the project. Through all the various challenges of getting a project built, we tried to clarify the design with each revision, while always seeking ways to be subtly inventive in the ways of making and creating opportunities to inhabit the building.

　The projects in this book share a chronology of our work since founding Turnbull Griffin Haesloop Architects, especially our houses. We are documenting our place in the lineage of Moore Lyndon Turnbull Whitaker and William Turnbull Associates and illustrating how Turnbull Griffin Haesloop's design sensibility refined the core values of honoring both people and place.

The Nature of Simplicity

Daniel P. Gregory

For Mary Griffin and Eric Haesloop and their design partners, especially Stefan Hastrup and Margaret Turnbull, whom I have known for nearly forty years, design involves expressing what I would call "the mechanics of simplicity." It is a process of exploration and refinement. Like their founding partner, the late William Turnbull Jr., they draw inspiration from architectural history—for example, early modern work by William Wurster, Alvar Aalto, and Eero Saarinen—but are interested in a freer manipulation of the built form, and in the expression of environmental sustainability.

Wurster once described his point of view as follows: "When a hillside is given to me on which to place a house, I embrace it and do not long for a meadow; conversely, when a site comes on a meadow, I do not long for a hillside." Mary and Eric do this and more: they look for ways their architecture can make a site more visible. To this end, they reinvent iconic architectural features—such as elegantly proportioned gables, overhangs, window walls, and outdoor rooms—while adding energy efficiency to make imaginative structures and settings that are both familiar and fresh.

This duality in their work reminds me of what the late San Francisco sculptor Adaline Kent, whose abstract work riffed on aspects of the Sierra landscape, once said: "I like to make things that if you come upon them in the half-light of evening, you say: 'Excuse me.'" Obviously, you don't say "Excuse me" when you see a house or academic building by TGH, but you pause to look again. You know it…and you don't. Here then is a brief primer on reading their work.

The house beside an aspen grove on a high mountain meadow in Walden, Colorado, with dazzling distant views toward Steamboat Springs, is monumental and modest at the same time. When I visited Connor Creek Ranch, I was struck by the contrast between the warmth and intimacy of the interior and the alpine majesty of the

Connor Creek Ranch, Walden, Colorado

exterior. The house presents as a series of nested boxes. The outermost is a two-story gable, grandly scaled to the mountain landscape, that extends past the house proper through a window wall to shelter and frame a stone porch with an outdoor fireplace, an inglenook turned inside-out. Inside, the ground floor is mostly a book-lined living room and galley kitchen, with a smaller master bedroom and bath upstairs. Walk from the living room onto the stone porch and you enter a Rocky Mountain diorama. It is house-as-theater, bringing to mind Shakespeare's famous stage direction from *The Winter's Tale*: "Exit, pursued by a bear." (Though I saw no bears while I was there.)

The gable that, as Mary says, "fronts and claims" its setting, is a key element in several other TGH designs. Their Commons for the Branson School in Ross, California, is situated at one end of a small valley and overlooks a playing field. The double-height glass gable of the student center rises from the center of a blank, board-formed concrete wall extending into upslopes on either side. Utility spaces and parking are hidden at the rear. The building acts as a sort of reconstituted dam or sluice gate, at once holding back the clutter of food preparation while modulating—and showcasing—the ebb and flow of student interaction both within it and before it.

TGH's Portola Valley house for an animator, graphic designer, and botanist and her husband, an inventor and computer science professor, is a laboratory for living with nature. The site is a swale with forest views to the south. Three wings angle around a round stone plant island like contemporary Conestoga wagons circling a campfire. Entry is beside a gabled workshop wing and into the verdant central courtyard. The workshop roof cantilevers over the entry path, marking the way through the courtyard to the front door. Deer are welcome here, thanks to the client's careful selection of plants that are resistant to munching. At left, under a flat living roof is a computer lab and crafts studio. Straight ahead is the

Branson School, Ross, California

Portola Valley Garden

Hupomone, Petaluma, California

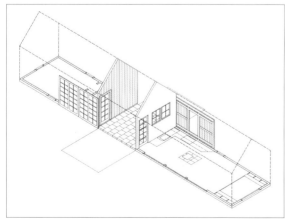

Axonometric, Teviot Springs, Calistoga, California

front door and the gabled two-story living/dining space, with an open kitchen tucked under the master suite. The great rooms' window wall rises the full two stories—as at Walden and Branson—and opens to a south-facing porch, flooding the interior with light and life. This is where the couple relax when they are not busy in their maker spaces.

In the rolling farmland of Petaluma, California, lies an especially evocative TGH design. Called Hupomone Ranch, using a Greek word for endurance, it takes a characteristic barn shape: high central gable flanked by shed-roofed wings or "saddlebags." The difference is in its transparency and in the flush-mounted vertical boards painted a glowing white. Set in the middle of a small valley, it commands the vista and draws your eye. The entry is through a lens, lightly, if you will. Clear glass barn doors slide open to a great room whose far wall, also glass, but now rising the full height of the house, frames and celebrates the long view down the valley. Nothing distracts from that view, and from the sense of a unified whole. As Eric explains, "We spend a lot of time to make things look really minimal." In other words, every detail has been carefully wrought and refined down to an almost elemental state. For example: the roof is as thin as it can be; the front upstairs window is precisely at the center of the facade; and the big rectangles of wood-framed glass that are the barn doors become abstract modern paintings when slid across the vertical boards of the facade. Meet a modern apotheosis of the barn, with the enduring, even classic, presence of a Greek temple.

I like to imagine that Gertrude Stein might have said, "A barn is a barn is a barn is a barn," instead of "a rose is a rose is a rose." That begins to get at how Mary and Eric have instilled new meaning into barn shapes. For them a barn can also be a dogtrot: two rooms separated by a covered walkway, a vernacular house type found in the South. At Teviot, Mary Griffin and Bill Turnbull's own gabled vineyard retreat near Calistoga, the covered open space is an outdoor dining room between the kitchen/living space and the bedroom wing. Nearby, the house TGH designed for Mary's sister-in-law, Margaret Turnbull, and her husband, Hank Jones, varies the theme. It appears to be a small barn containing a living room between a galley kitchen on one side and a bedroom on the other. But when the big sliding glass doors centered on front and rear are open, the living room becomes the dogtrot. It turns out you can have your barn and a breezeway, too!

A larger, more dramatic version with flat roofs, some of which are planted, is for a vacation house near Glen Ellen, on a gradually sloping site overlooking a pond. The scheme is composed of three key elements: lower kitchen and sleeping units skinned in horizontal boards and covered in living roofs, a higher living room ringed with clerestories, and a spacious covered entrance terrace/outdoor living room (the dogtrot). The high flat roof over the living room extends across the entry terrace, anchored by the chimney of the outdoor fireplace and passing over part of the guest suite on the other side. It ties the composition together visually while focusing views down to the pond. The design vividly celebrates your arrival in a landscape of ease and freedom.

At Stinson Beach, the clients asked TGH to design a building on an oceanfront site where the family's original house by William Wurster had burned down. They wanted something up to date but with a sense of history. So Mary and Eric turned to another Wurster design, for an oceanside site at Aptos in 1937, for inspiration. That house, famous as an early exemplar of Bay Region Modernism, was a simple two-story central mass flanked on the beach side by two small glass-fronted, open-air pavilions, which provided sitting areas that protected from wind yet were open to the sun. At Stinson, FEMA rules require living spaces to be on "breakaway construction," one floor above the ground, so the entire

Coyote Camp, Calistoga, California

Sonoma Retreat dogtrot, Sonoma, California

Clark Residence, William Wurster, Architect, Aptos, California

Stinson Beach Oceanfront, Residence, Stinson Beach, California

H-shaped house sits on wood posts with rod bracing like a fishing pier. Now, the two glazed wings projecting toward the sand are sitting rooms with the primary bedroom behind one and a wind-sheltered deck behind the other. Their shed roofs angle upward, capturing sunlight and ocean views. The living/dining area lies at the center of the H, and a sliding window wall opens to a deck and the beach below. Seen from the side, the house resembles an angular wooden wave rolling toward the shore.

Other shed roof designs appear throughout the TGH portfolio, but an especially dramatic example is their house at Atherton, California, that reads as a pavilion whose roof angles upward to open the house toward a small pond at the rear. The drama is in this rear wall, which, in the main part of the house, consists of eight elegantly proportioned sliding window walls running from the great room at one end to the living room at the other. They open the house to a slender concrete deck that appears to float over the pond. The thinness of the deck, the large scale of the sliding doors, and the upsweep of the roof combine to dramatize the water view. House and waterscape become extensions of each other. When I was there, standing in one of the doorways, I felt I had wandered into a compact, modern, and very private national park.

This brings me to a design that is both parklike and more abstract: a house in Kentfield on a steep slope with views across a canyon to San Francisco Bay in the distance. This U-shaped house, mostly covered in a living roof, wraps around a central pool courtyard that is seemingly dug into the hill. A deck along the opposite side of the house opens the main living spaces to the view. The courtyard side of the house feels cave-like, reminiscent of a modern Mesa Verde cliff dwelling. The smooth rear wall of the courtyard traces the curve of the slope behind and above it. Three angled light-scoops, or sheds, rise through the living roof to define and brighten the living

Atherton Retreat, California

Marin Hillside, Kentfield, California

room, kitchen/dining room, and primary bedroom. The planted roof functions visually as an artful extension of the hillside, as if the slope has flattened into a meadow. The house becomes a sculptural extension of the site.

Indeed, to highjack a phrase from Mary Griffin's preface, "framing or revealing" key site features is always a primary goal—which sometimes means that structures deconstruct and then recombine with the site, as at their isolated Healdsburg Knoll house with views to distant slopes and valleys. Built for a family that loves outdoor cooking for large family gatherings, this house embodies a phrase that Bill Turnbull often referenced from Berkeley's Hillside Club yearbook of 1908: "Hillside architecture is landscape gardening around a few rooms in case of rain."

Those rooms are what Eric has called "saddlebags around a void." Put another way, the house is itself the void—centered on the sheltered outdoor cooking platform—while kitchen, living room, entry portal, family sleeping wing, and infinity-edge pool dissolve into the edges of the knoll. The day I visited, I stood by the pool and looked back toward the compound. The deconstructed elements seemed to reassemble before my eyes just as David Wakely's wide-angle shot from that very point shows. The left-to-right progression from hillside to liquid (pool), to solid (living room), to framed volume (kitchen), to framed voids (cooking platform and portal), back to solid (family sleeping wing), and then back to hillside, forms a marvelous architectural topology. The house has become its landscape, a panorama of place.

To read the designs of TGH is to witness gifted imagination at work. Their structures make us see the world in new ways. As landscape architect Walter Hood once said about the Teviot retreat: "There is so much bigness in the smallness of it." It turns out that what might appear to be so simple—isn't.

Healdsburg Knoll, Sonoma, California

Stinson Beach Oceanfront House

Tipping to the views

Located at Stinson Beach in Marin County, this house replaces the clients' beloved William Wurster house that burned down on the site. They requested we design the new house to capture the spirit of the original 1960s house while meeting all the current seismic codes and FEMA requirements for buildings constructed in vulnerable coastal zones. While the original house was low-lying and tucked into the dunes, the current codes required us to raise the floor level of the new house almost a full story since any nonstructural part of the building that touches the ground must be designed to break away and let water flow through in the case of a tsunami. We studied other Wurster projects for clues and inspiration. The challenges of the site forced us to innovate and design a house within the strict height limit that was perched to meet the codes but still settled on the ground. The rectangular plan with cutouts for decks and stairs is enclosed under a roof that folds to allow shed roofs to tip up to views of the Marin Hills to the north and of the Pacific Ocean to the south. The X bracing of the elevated structure ties the building to the ground. To allow the clients choices about inhabiting this dramatic site, we shaped the building volumes under the folding roof to create a variety of wind-sheltered outdoor spaces. Facing the ocean, a pair of open-air covered pavilions frame the front deck with wide steps, connecting down to the beach.

Original house that burned down, by Wurster Bernardi & Emmons, Architects, Stinson Beach, California

Diagram of San Andreas fault line

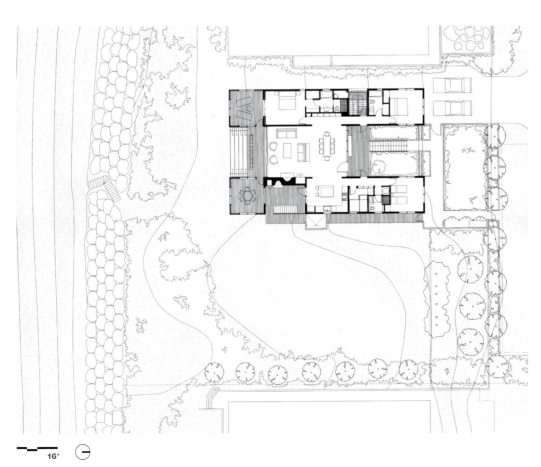

16'

25 STINSON BEACH OCEANFRONT HOUSE

TURNBULL GRIFFIN HAESLOOP ARCHITECTS

Sausalito Remodel

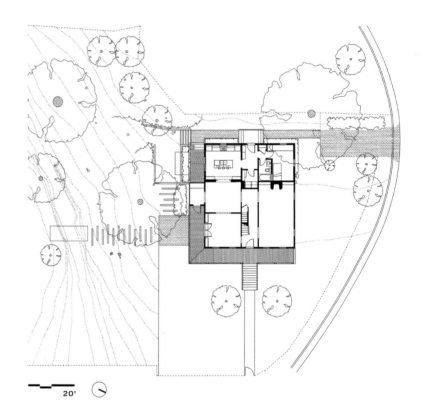

Infusing light

Built in 1869, this white clapboard Carpenter Gothic house is the oldest surviving dwelling constructed in Sausalito. The house sits above a perennial creek and faces east out toward San Francisco Bay. The historic building features a classic foursquare house plan, high ceilings, and porches wrapping two sides. The kitchen, originally located in a detached building for fire concerns, had been relocated into one of the four first floor rooms. Sensitive to the historically significant original structure, we approached the redesign by demolishing an attached shed addition and replacing it with a shed-roofed extension that allowed the makeshift kitchen to move out of the historic house. The new structure uses slightly different siding, fenestration, and roofing to distinguish it from the historic house. Our design goal was to respect the bones and character of the original structure while infusing light into previously dark rooms. The new kitchen is roofed with translucent panels, allowing warm southern light to fill the interior. Large axial openings are added to link and open the original rooms to one another and the landscape beyond. An added deck off the kitchen leads down to a brick-paved terrace overlooking the creek. The sensitive renovation transforms the interior into a series of light-filled flowing spaces, while preserving the historic qualities of the house.

Gardner house, 1869, Sausalito, California

Old kitchen location

New kitchen location

20'

35 SAUSALITO REMODEL

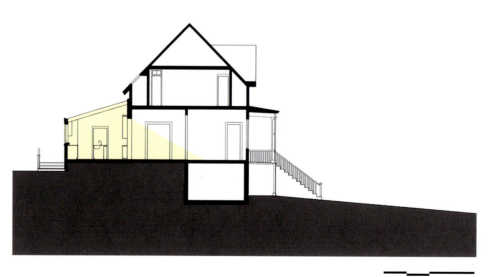

TURNBULL GRIFFIN HAESLOOP ARCHITECTS

Connor Creek Ranch

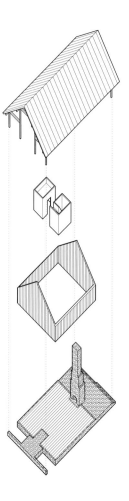

*Sheltering roof
in a vast landscape*

Set on a spectacular plateau at an elevation of 8,000 feet on Colorado's North Slope, the site for this house is part of a working ranch with expansive fields, stands of aspen, and distant views to Steamboat Springs. Our challenge was to make a small program hold its own in the grand landscape. We formed a loosely arranged compound by siting three small buildings—house, guesthouse, and garage—along an almost level contour, following the edge of an aspen grove. The clients, fascinated with small houses, requested modestly sized living spaces for both philosophical and practical reasons: they wanted to use each space in the house every day and minimize energy consumption. We oversized the gable roofs of the house and garage to respond to the vast landscape. The expansive roof of the main house shelters the compact interior program and creates a generous protected outdoor porch with a large stone fireplace that looks across the plateau to the mountains beyond. Under the roof, the house is an almost square plan with zones of space created by inserting two white clapboard square volumes. One houses the stair and the other the pantry and dressing area above. The cubes organize the interior spaces, creating a sense of nesting under the big roof. These interior structures pull apart and open to the high ceiling above, creating a path on axis with the stone fireplace. The living spaces surround the cubes with low ceilings at the clients' request. The house responds to its severe winters by sitting on a stone plinth under the steep roofs with big sheltering overhangs.

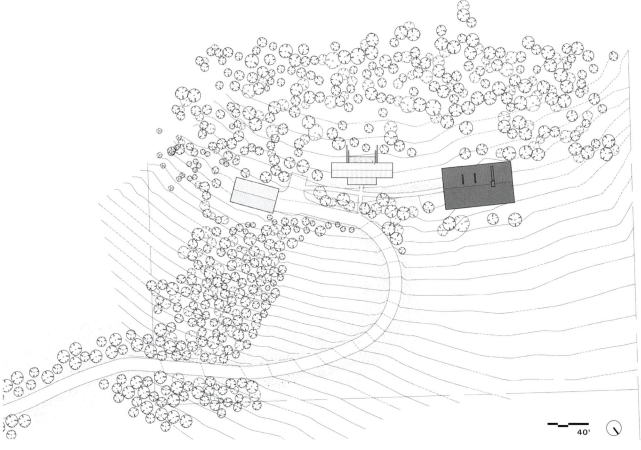

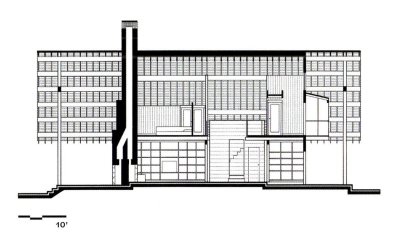

43 CONNOR CREEK RANCH

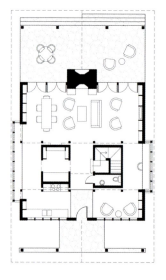
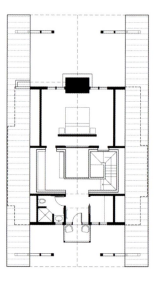

Sea Ranch Bluff

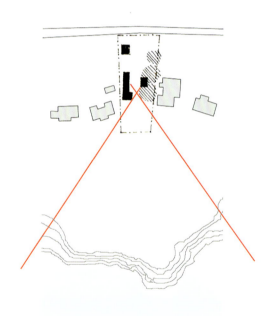

Stepping aside to let the landscape flow through

The Bluff House site was one of the last unbuilt oceanfront lots along a road at the southern end of The Sea Ranch. When we first visited the site, the lot felt so narrow we assumed it was the side yard of the neighboring house. On this sliver of a site, we separated the program into several building volumes that edge the site and create a central axial procession that unfolds down toward the views of the meadow and Pacific Ocean beyond. Two simple wooden shed-roofed buildings edge a wooden deck that frames the view to the ocean, making the landscape center stage on the site. For quiet and privacy, we sited the primary bedroom structure behind a mature cypress tree. Across the deck, in the main house, the living space steps down and opens out with a generous wooden corner bay.

At The Sea Ranch, most houses push forward of their neighbors to maximize their ocean views. In our design, the central outdoor space created by separating the buildings allowed us to pull the Bluff House back from the string of neighboring houses. When we visited the staking of the house prior to the start of construction, we realized we could site the house back an additional ten feet from the oceanfront and the neighbors and improve the views. By organizing the architectural concept into two distinct structures, sited in relation to the stand of trees along the edge of the lot, a private sanctuary with diagonal views across the clients' own lot and out to the ocean was created within The Sea Ranch's existing, developed landscape.

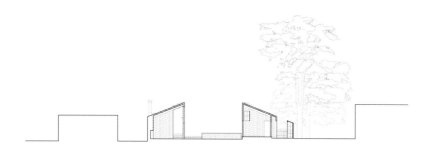

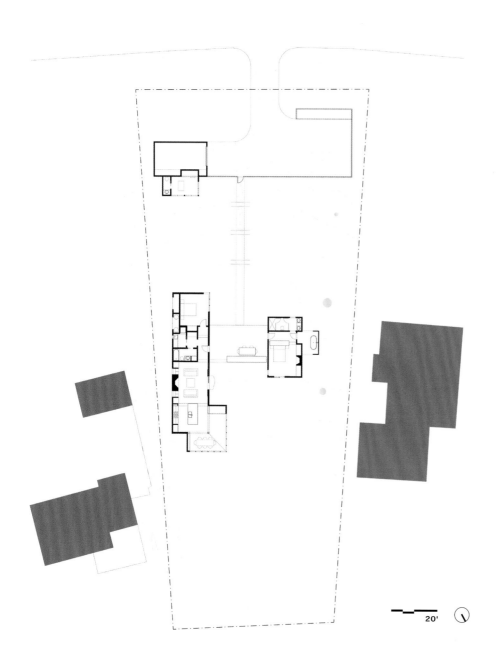

TURNBULL GRIFFIN HAESLOOP ARCHITECTS

TURNBULL GRIFFIN HAESLOOP ARCHITECTS

Santa Lucia Preserve

Anchoring with earth walls

Located southwest of Carmel Valley, the Santa Lucia Preserve transformed a 20,000-acre coastal ranch dating from the 1830s into a planned conservation community. Master-planned for house sites surrounded by tracts of open space, each parcel has a strict building envelope designed to preserve the natural habitat and native landscape. Our clients' parcel sits just above the preserve's historic hacienda and barns, surrounded by open grassland below and an oak forest above and behind the site. They asked us to create a family gathering place that recaptured some of the feeling of a beloved Adirondacks camp they had once owned, by incorporating log construction.

Our design solution addresses the transition in the landscape, by organizing the program into a series of separate buildings that engage different qualities of the site and the topography of the hill. The main building fronts out with a broad porch facing the equestrian center and valley below. The kitchen opens onto a grove of oaks, providing shaded outdoor space. The landscape flows through the covered exterior walkway that steps up the hill to the bedroom cabins that occupy the secluded upper part of the site.

In response to the owners' interest in log construction, we used logs as structural elements to support the exterior walkway, to hold up the second floor of the main house, and to frame the front porch. The primary exterior walls of the main house are constructed of sprayed earth, using soil from the site. The mass of the sprayed earth walls, in combination with strategically placed operable windows, allows the house to be naturally cooled. Other sustainable design choices include certified siding and decking, both exterior and interior. The floors and beams are constructed with reclaimed wood. The use of the earth, logs, reclaimed wood, and corrugated zinc roof reinforce the diagram, creating a compound that captures and complements the magical and varied qualities of the site.

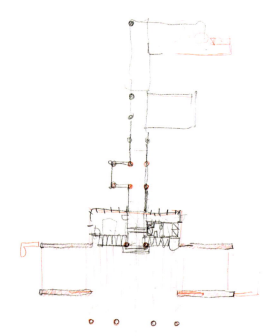

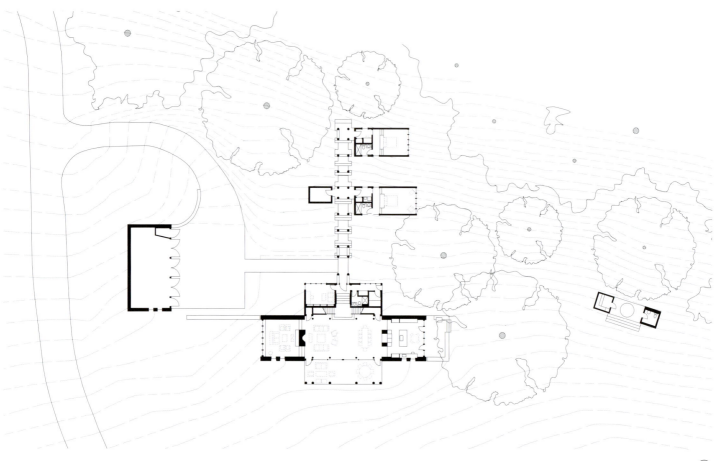

TURNBULL GRIFFIN HAESLOOP ARCHITECTS

Lake Tahoe Retreat

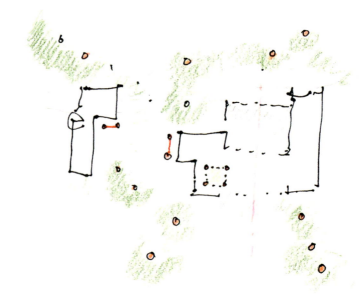

Among the trees

Located on the Nevada side of Lake Tahoe, this two-building compound was created as a gathering place for four sisters and their extended families. At Cascade Beach on the northern tip of Lake Tahoe, the sisters had grown up vacationing at a family retreat centered around a stone William Wurster–designed lodge. They purchased a property on the eastern shore of the lake with views out over a meadow to the lake and backing up to a forest. When designing the new compound, we were asked to recall the qualities of the Wurster buildings. Because of strict planning requirements for construction along the shores of the lake, the buildings follow the footprint of the original 1950s house and garage, preserving all the existing pine and fir trees. The two structures have entry porches supported by log columns that face each other across the entry path. The siting of the main house forms a wind-protected courtyard that embraces the hill with a small retaining wall to shape the space. The living room features large sliding doors on either side of the space to create an enclosed pass-through connecting the back courtyard, the living room, and the front lawn, with its views across the meadow to the lake.

   Since Lake Tahoe sustains heavy snow loads in the winter, the forms of the buildings feature simple standing-seam zinc gable roofs that shed the snow and covered entries at the gable ends. The sidewalls are sheathed with cedar shingles. On the interior, the house is heavily insulated on exterior walls, which are clad with vertical grain Douglas fir boards. Also heavily insulated, the ceilings of the one-story portions of the house are Sheetrock revealed from the sidewalls. The dining area is defined by four log columns forming an aedicula, with the ceiling framing exposed and lit by a skylight. In the kitchen, which has a second story above, the ceiling rafters are again revealed. The compound merges into the Sierra landscape with both structures looking out to views of Lake Tahoe through a sheltering screen of mature trees.

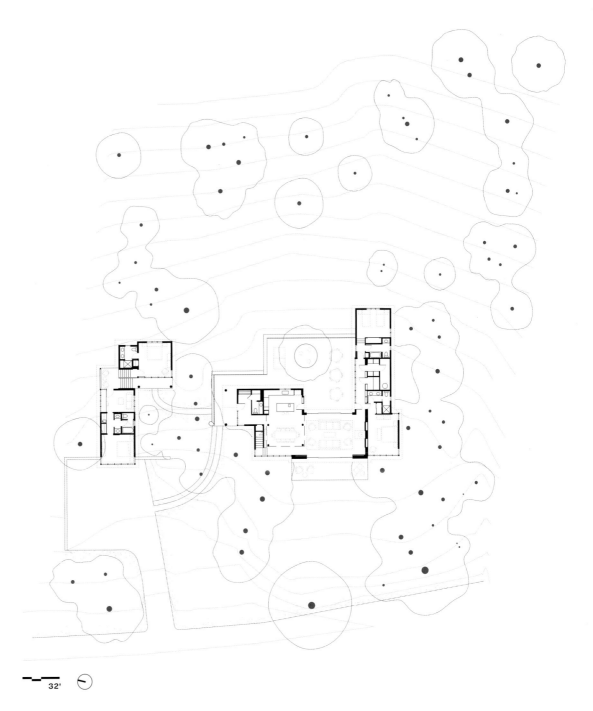

Sebastopol Camp

Bridging between redwoods

On an unusually narrow site near Occidental, in Sonoma County, we designed a house for two graphic designers. The sloping site featured clusters of redwood trees and broad views of coastal hills and forests to the north. The parcel of land stretches along the access drive to a neighbor's property. The design solution is a long narrow house that bridges over a dip in the land with wooden decks at either end, sitting at grade. Anchored by stands of mature redwood trees along the same contour, a path leads down to the pool compound on one side and to the studio/garage on the other.

The defining design move of the main house is a continuous glass facade that looks north out to the expansive view of distant hills. On the entry side, a horizontal cedar rainscreen wall shields the house's interior from the driveway and road above. A band of high clerestory windows runs the length of the house, allowing southern light to flow in. The form of the building is a shed sloping down to the north. Yet, as you enter, the roof pops up over the dining area, creating a dormer that gestures to the view. Although the main house is only 1,700 square feet, the open floor plan creates a spacious feeling. The closed exterior opens on the interior to a world of wood and glass with Sheetrock dividers. The walls and casework that define the exterior shape of the house are Douglas fir with Douglas fir beams and decking framing the ceiling. White Sheetrock interior walls float off the exterior to divide the spaces while allowing views the entire length of the house. The bedroom and bath have sliding doors that disappear into the walls, and the long southern wall bookcase houses the clients' wonderful art objects. The exterior is clad in cedar siding with a metal roof. The outbuildings step along the contours to create a camp of linked structures sited among the trees.

Pool

Main house

Garage/studio

32'

TURNBULL GRIFFIN HAESLOOP ARCHITECTS

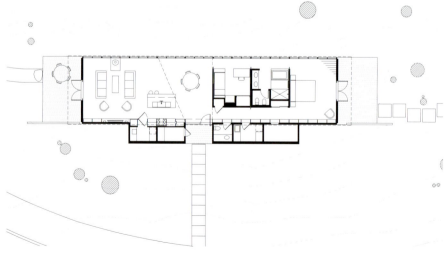

Grace Magill Arts and Science Building, Burke's School

Responding to the context

Burke's School occupies a 3.5-acre campus in the affluent Sea Cliff neighborhood of San Francisco, just a block away from the Pacific Ocean. The site, a former bus yard, is a long narrow interior parcel with access only from one end. Over the years, nearby property owners restricted development of the campus due to traffic concerns. Sited away from neighboring houses, the Grace Magill Arts and Science Building fills an underutilized corner site at the end of the linear campus to create a learning center for upper-grade students. The building backs onto the golf course of Lincoln Park, a 100-acre coastal recreation area. To break up the scale, the facade facing the park and the neighbors to the west is articulated with bay windows and natural wood siding. On the opposite side, the building faces out onto a generous outdoor play yard. Because of planning restrictions, the new structure could not claim the end of the long campus.

Our design solution features an overscale porch that steps forward to mark the entry. Exterior stairs and covered walkways along the long facade create an engaging terminus. The upper walkway offers a narrow view out to the Pacific Ocean. The residential scale of the building addresses the neighbors' concerns, while the design of the porch defines the end of the campus. The two-story, 9,500-square-foot building includes science classrooms, flexible teaching spaces for music and drama, an art studio, and a multipurpose meeting room. All spaces feature windows looking into the park as well as out to campus. Within a strict budget with many site constraints, this small building responds elegantly to its varied contexts—the campus, the park, and the neighborhood.

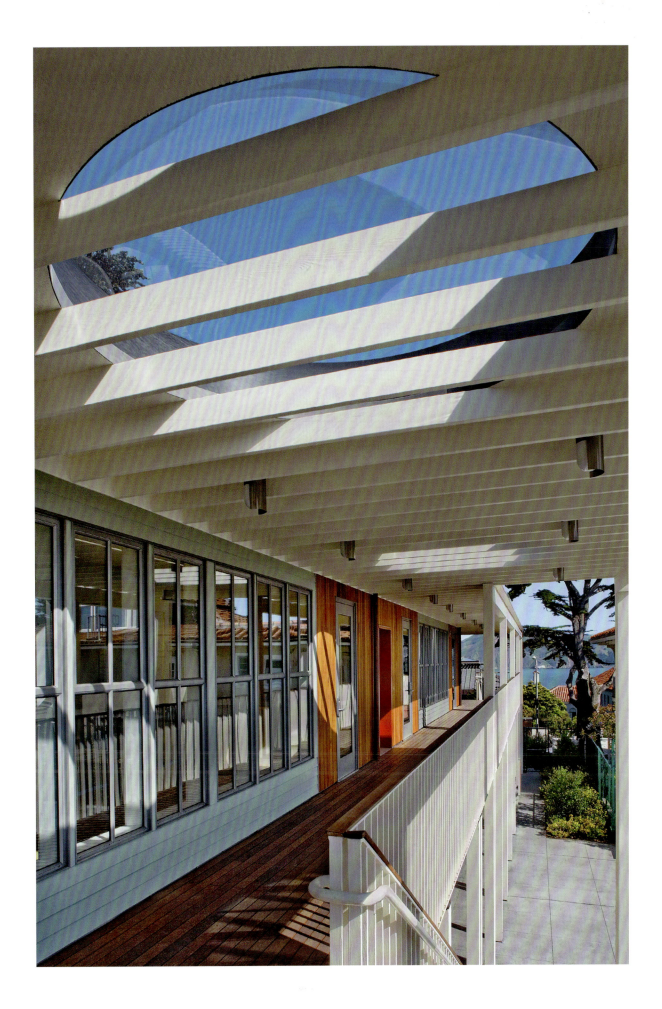

Atherton Retreat

Floating in the garden

Located on the peninsula south of San Francisco, this house sits on an internal suburban flag lot accessed by a long driveway. The clients had lived in the 1950s house on the site for many years, which, due to structural problems, required replacement. Demolishing their original house, the clients asked to preserve the mature landscaping that included a small pond in the middle of the site. Enthusiasts of year-round, outdoor dining and entertaining, they desired a house that opens to the landscape with as many outdoor rooms as possible. We decided to expand the pond and divide the program into four buildings—a main house, a study, a pool house, and a garage—all ringing the edge of the site and focusing inward on the pond, garden, and swimming pool.

The main house on the entry side parallels the car court; the house becomes the threshold between the entry and the private interior world within. The living spaces flow to the pond's edge under the tipped-up butterfly roof with a dramatic overhang. Casework dividers create spaces within. The stone floors of the interior flow out to the terraces, blurring the line between indoors and out. Large sliding glass barn doors are custom designed to provide expansive openings that can be screened. The roofs conceal photovoltaic and solar hot water panels. In the mild Atherton climate, the owners chose to keep the house open to the outdoors and passively cooled with a combination of overhangs, shades, and operable windows. The house, clad with stained cedar boards, also features many green building materials, including high fly-ash concrete.

The study building is located across the terrace from the main house, looking back at the pond. A path then leads up through the garden to the pool and guesthouse with an outdoor kitchen. The new compound offers the clients many choices of how to occupy this unique environment, making their residence feel like a vacation retreat.

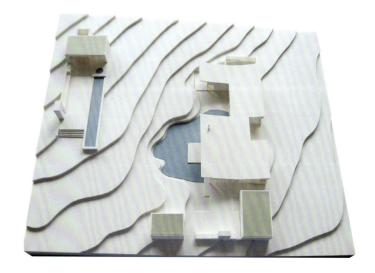

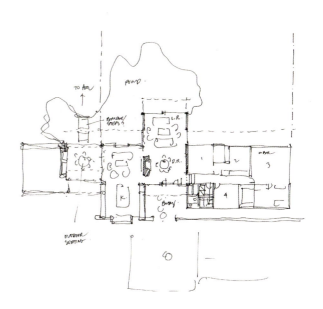

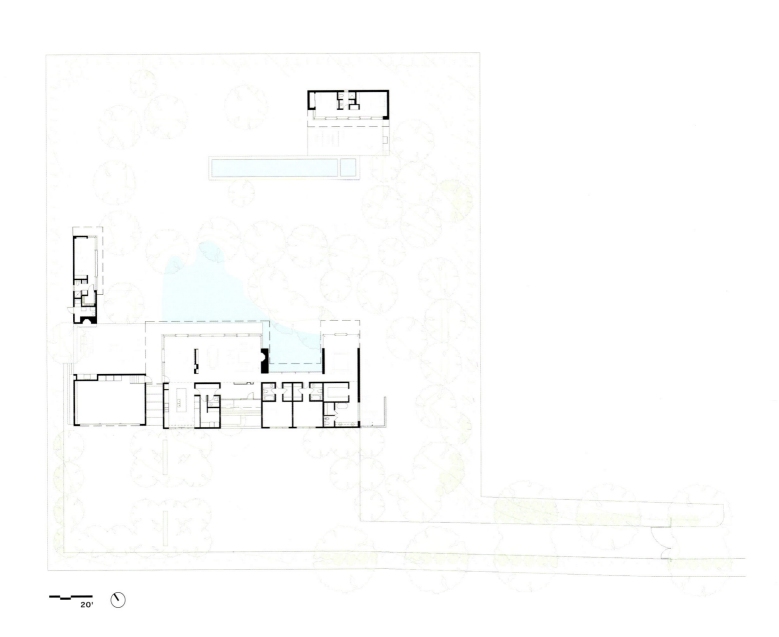

101 ATHERTON RETREAT

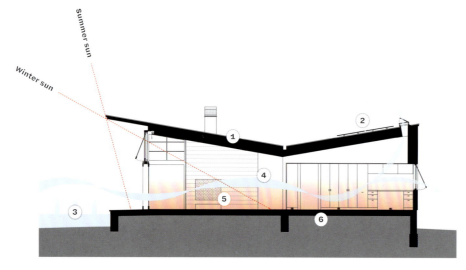

Climate strategy
1. R-45 insulation
2. Photovoltaics
3. Evaporative cooling
4. Cross ventilation
5. Radiant heating
6. Thermal mass

Turnbull Griffin Haesloop Houses at The Sea Ranch
Donlyn Lyndon

Condominium One, MLTW, Moore Lyndon Turnbull Whitaker Architects, The Sea Ranch, California

All Turnbull Griffin Haesloop houses at The Sea Ranch are especially well-suited to their sites. They carry the marks of exceptional professional skill in the creation of appropriate building forms, the artful detailing of each element, and the planning that underlies their positions in space. To their owners and guests, these houses offer a range of places and conditions to inhabit, inviting relaxed movement and rest. They glow with light from many sources: skylights and high windows and from the windows of linked rooms that open into one another and out to the landscape, near and far. As elements in the community landscape, these buildings sit gracefully and calmly among neighboring houses and trees.

The TGH work represents, as well, something more: the living continuity of the legacy of William Turnbull's contribution to the very idea of The Sea Ranch as a place. As partners with Charles Moore and Richard Whitaker in the then-newly formed firm MLTW (Moore Lyndon Turnbull Whitaker), Bill and I worked together frequently and intensely, the four of us bringing varied inclinations, favorite recollections, and inspirations to the tasks at hand. Of the group, Bill was always the one most attuned to the site, the one to whom we turned for the most acute insights regarding how to fit our work into the land, of which it became a part.

Those of us in the MLTW partnership learned to incorporate many of these qualities into the work of other firms, as we went our separate ways, lured by teaching and administrative opportunities at diverse universities. Bill Turnbull, instead, was determined to stay put, in his office at Pier 1½ in San Francisco, with a practice that included civic buildings and many fine houses. There he honed his understanding of the landscape of The Sea Ranch on many sites.

At The Sea Ranch, Bill Turnbull's buildings stewarded the land to support a respectful involvement with nature, not motivated by agriculture and production but developed as places of observation and enjoyment. This meant finding the proper places on the land, positioning buildings so that they appear as part of the landscape, establishing platforms for outlook and pleasant living. Each part of The Sea Ranch has its own special character to be nurtured, sometimes with small courts and gardens, sometimes with buildings that sit on sweeping slopes, or with structures that settle quietly among segments of forest.

The San Francisco pier is also where Mary Griffin and Eric Haesloop began to learn these insights through their work with Bill at William Turnbull Associates (WTA). Mary had been my student, teaching assistant, and professional collaborator at MIT. She met Bill though gatherings with me and eventually she moved from Washington, DC, where she worked with George Hartman at Hartman-Cox Architects, learning the art of contextual design on projects ranging from houses to museums, to San Francisco to marry Bill in 1985 and to work with him at WTA. Also in 1985, Eric moved west from New Haven, where he had worked with César Pelli Associates and studied with Charles Moore at Yale, to join WTA. It was with Bill that Mary and Eric learned the subtleties of siting buildings gracefully in the land and building with wood.

Anderson Residence, The Sea Ranch, California

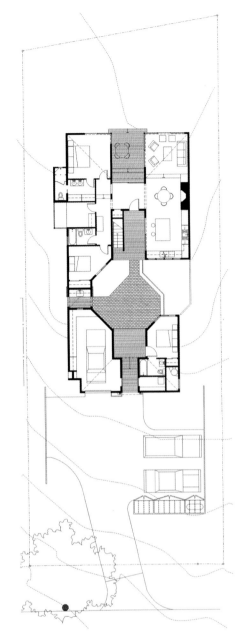

Cassani Residence, The Sea Ranch, California

They each brought their own skills to the team—Mary's vested interest in graceful rationality, imagination, and critical insight and Eric's ability to read sites and design inventive responses. After twelve years of collaboration, Bill's death in 1997 left Mary and Eric with the daunting task of reimagining the firm and forging ahead as Turnbull Griffin Haesloop to begin a new chapter.

Turnbull Griffin Haesloop is distinguished by the firm's collaborative creativity, the exacting simplicity of the designs, and the naturally restful siting of the buildings. Margaret Turnbull, the gifted interior designer who had long collaborated with her brother Bill, continued to enhance TGH projects. Mary and Eric were also joined by the talented designer Stefan Hastrup, who had studied with Bill when he was a visiting critic at Yale and who became a TGH principal in 2001. The places they have made are thoroughly engaging. By examining five TGH houses, we will see that all are set within different aspects of The Sea Ranch landscape, continuing while also extending Bill's original Sea Ranch ethos.

The Cassani Residence entryway, for instance, sited along the bluff at the north end of The Sea Ranch, illustrates how a sequence of courtyard and interior spaces join with the greater landscape. Occupants always understand where they are within the plan through the design of sight lines and vistas, guiding how they may move through the spaces, recognizing places of rest and enjoyment.

The Sea Ranch Meadow I house resides peacefully in the corner of a meadow near a grove of trees, harboring

Sea Ranch Meadow I Residence, The Sea Ranch, California

Sea Ranch Bluff Residence, The Sea Ranch, California

an outdoor room within the larger octagonal form. The main living spaces surround and open out to this sunny, wind-protected deck, their openings taking in views of the meadow, a hedgerow, and the Pacific Ocean beyond. Descending from the wood deck are soft, grass-covered earth steps, retained by risers made of thin steel plates. Viewed in plan, the house appears as an intersection of simple geometries: a square that is missing one corner, filled in by the octagonal shape that is the deck, oriented outward to large-plate glass doors opening out from interior spaces. The dramatic plane of the roof rises from a shallow pitch over the entry and service rooms, then peaks over the living room. The house is screened by trees from the road, offering privacy from the public entrance, yet wide open to the magnificent natural setting and sea beyond.

 For the Sea Ranch Bluff house the main forms face each other across a large wood-planked platform. The two buildings of different sizes, yet shared intent, define the open space between them to become part of the sloping landscape's flow. Within the larger, longer building resides a large common area and one bedroom. Its linear length steps down the gentle grade, close to the ground. The glass-walled dining space extends out into the meadow. The living area surrounds a fireplace and wall of bookshelves. Sitting across a wooden terrace is the principal bedroom, tucked under a large old cypress tree and next to a row of pines. The small building higher up the slope shelters a studio and garage. These buildings nestle into the landscape, creating a

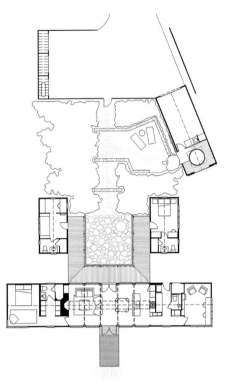

Boyd Residence, The Sea Ranch, California

harmonious and discrete composition, clad in vertical redwood siding.

The Boyd House and its three outbuildings (a garage and two guesthouses) enfold a court defining the place and its internal focus. TGH's gabled vernacular forms, a legacy of Bill Turnbull's influence, infuse the spaces with an intentional informality, a rustic feel that is at once orderly and minimalist. The building blocks arranged around the courtyard are connected by a colonnade of round, wooden columns sheltered by a glass roof. The symmetry of the centered doors and windows appears an abstraction upon first glance, then conveys a sense of calm after some contemplation. The longest block opens out to the powerful ocean, grounded by the long, central common room. It is a bright and meticulously crafted space, framed at one end by a shallow brick Rumford fireplace and the kitchen's elegant Douglas fir cabinetry at the other, bringing a golden warmth and resolve to the space. The principal bedroom occupies the private north end and a window-wrapped study absorbs the sun at the south end. A continuous skylight at the roof ridge infuses shifting light patterns through the exposed rafters and tie beams, dancing around walls and surfaces throughout the day. Two smaller buildings, sited perpendicular to the main house, provide ancillary spaces for guests. TGH's engagement of exceptional design, materials and craft lends the Boyd house its naturally breathtaking dimension.

The materials that are used to form these structures and spaces are chosen to be appropriate to their location

Skyfall Residence, The Sea Ranch, California

Sea Ranch Meadow II and Sea Ranch Meadow I, The Sea Ranch, California

and the uses they enfold. As wood has become more precious and is fire prone, TGH has explored innovative materials such as cement panels for the walls and roof of the Skyfall house, saving wood for special areas where people interact directly with the building. In all these houses, internal passages between blocks of rooms almost always reach to the outside, giving a fine sense of the whole place. Structural members are often present, defining and animating the spaces, not insistently seeking attention, but quietly explaining how it all comes together and demonstrating the investment in craft by all involved in making the place.

Turnbull Griffin Haesloop has developed a vocabulary of forms that gives special pleasures and offers lively incidents, while working within The Sea Ranch's established design guidelines, traditions that have evolved across more than fifty years to direct individual building design into a coherent affinity throughout the community. The built work of TGH exists within these guidelines and intentions, giving it special relevance through creating structures that not only fit their place but have a studied, quiet, and settled elegance. They offer new insights with their explorations of materials that better address fire safety and have greater endurance to weathering. All these qualities cohere beautifully in the work of Turnbull Griffin Haesloop at The Sea Ranch. They continue to form instructive examples of what architecture can be in this beautiful and special place.

Sea Ranch Meadow I

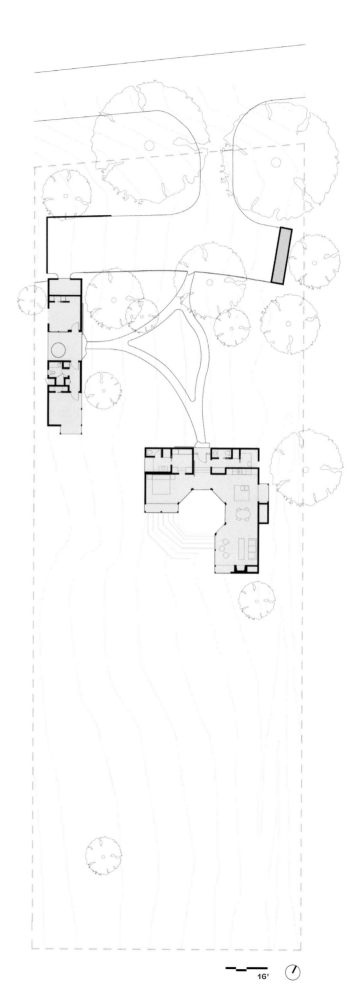

Shaping meadow views

Located at the southern end of The Sea Ranch on an infill lot, this 1,030-square-foot house and 550-square-foot guesthouse create a threshold in the larger landscape, between the contained space of the hedgerow and the open space of the meadow. Inspired by the earlier agricultural forms along the Northern California coast, this compound pairs the gable barn shape of the main house with the shed shape of the guesthouse. The buildings enclose a woodland garden that leads to the entry of the main house, where you step up into a passage and into the broad barn volume. The roof cuts away to shape an exterior octagonal deck that connects the open meadow to the center of the house. Grass-planted header steps spill down from the deck out into the meadow. The house is an open plan with a continuous band of windows and doors around the octagonal cutout to capture distant diagonal views of the Pacific coastline. By carving into the volume, the simple form of the barn becomes site-specific and spatially dynamic.

When wood was local and plentiful, early Sea Ranch houses often featured all-wood interiors. Our clients, inspired by Japanese design, asked us to rethink the use of interior wood and treat it as a precious commodity to be showcased. Layered materials reveal the steel and wood framing of the window wall. The perimeter interior walls of the barn are painted white. The exposed wood and steel construction occurs on the shaped walls and bays and in the exposed framing of the ceiling. Special areas, such as the breakfast nook, celebrate refined wood detailing.

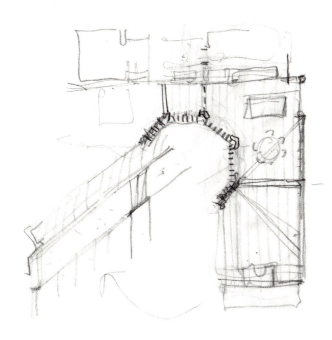

Sea Ranch Meadow II

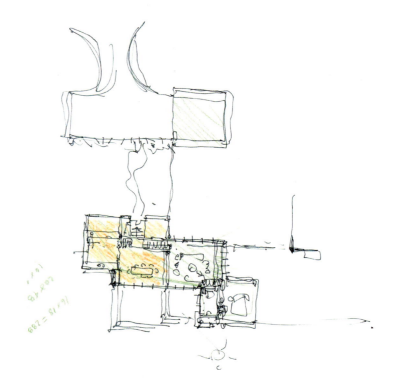

Sloping with the land

With a growing extended family, the owners of Sea Ranch Meadow I acquired the adjoining downhill lot and asked us to design a new main house and garage to complement the original compound built fifteen years earlier. The challenge became how to link the sites and make the two projects enhance one another. Ironically, the siting of Sea Ranch Meadow I included a guesthouse we carefully located to screen future development on the adjacent lot they now own. By removing a hot tub deck and cutting a passage through the guesthouse, an inviting gatehouse with a wood walkway now links the two parcels. With our own project as our context, we continued the exterior palette of the first house with updates for current energy efficiency goals. The forms of the two houses from the meadow view respond to one another, and, in the spirit of the original Sea Ranch Meadow design vision, they aggregate to be good neighbors. Sea Ranch Meadow II features a long shed roof gently sloping with the land up toward the first house. On the interior, the house steps up the hill with the contours.

   The main volume of the house—the living and dining areas—is designed to capture diagonal views though the space. It features high vertical windows to the north, looking up into the firs and large horizontal slide-away doors to the south, opening onto a deck with views toward the ocean. The new house allowed us to consider evolving ideas for making the house more energy efficient while also also exploring using wood in tectonic ways. For example, the cavity above the ceiling of the main spaces is superinsulated, and then sheathed with continuous shiplap cedar boards. The boards create warmth and texture as a counterpoint to the Sheetrock walls and stone floors. Carefully placed skylights and windows allow light to play upon these materials. For net-zero power usage, solar panels are subtly located on the sloped roof. Elegant and serene, Sea Ranch Meadow II creates a retreat for the design-sensitive clients amid family life.

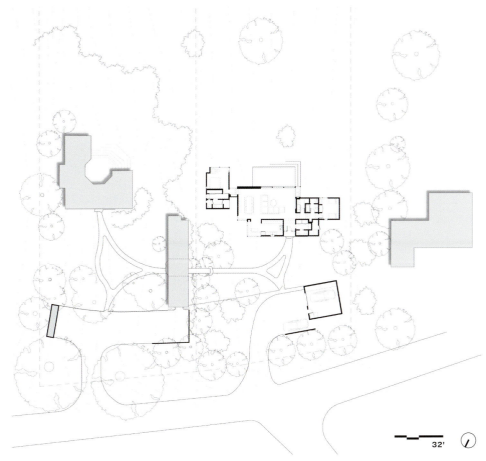

SEA RANCH MEADOW II

SEA RANCH MEADOW II

The Commons, Branson School

Claiming the center

Branson School, an independent high school, occupies seventeen acres of beautiful, hilly terrain in Ross, a residential community about twenty miles north of San Francisco. Many of the campus buildings are converted residences. The new 7,750-square-foot Commons building reclaims a boggy site located along the pedestrian path between the upper and lower campuses and transforms it to become the heart of the campus. The building claims its site and central status with a large transparent window wall that fronts onto an inviting terrace and lawn. The flanking support wings, sheltered under living roofs, merge into the adjacent hillsides with board-formed concrete walls.

Sited to maximize the southern exposure, the Commons building features large overhead doors that tip up to open onto a generous plaza for dining, meeting, and outdoor classes. Inside large box trusses made of reclaimed wood create an airy space that flows through to the serving area with a glazed wall above. The Commons provides spaces for large group events and dining inside and out, as well as smaller places for informal gatherings throughout the day offering students, faculty, and visitors a multiuse center. The building is certified LEED Platinum and features many sustainable strategies, including the living roof, daylighting, natural ventilation, solar collectors, and pervious paving with a dispersant pond.

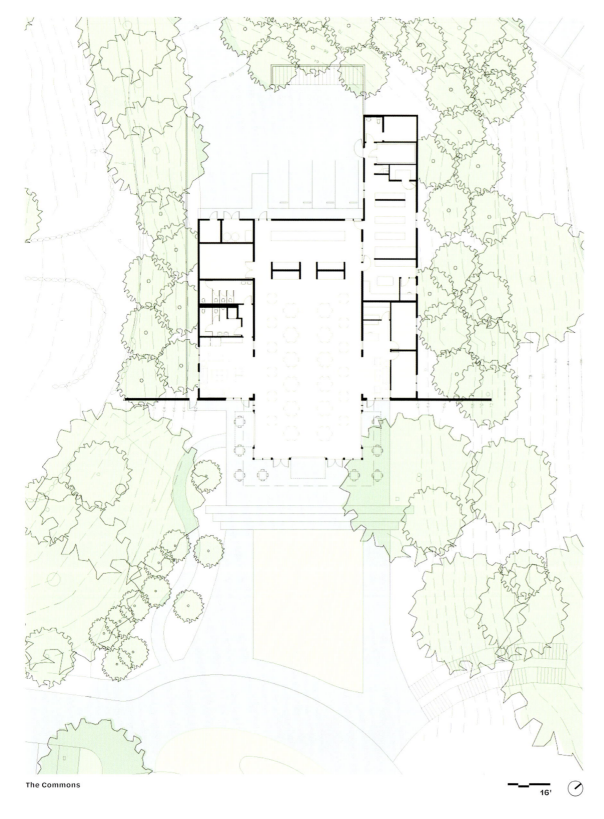

The Commons

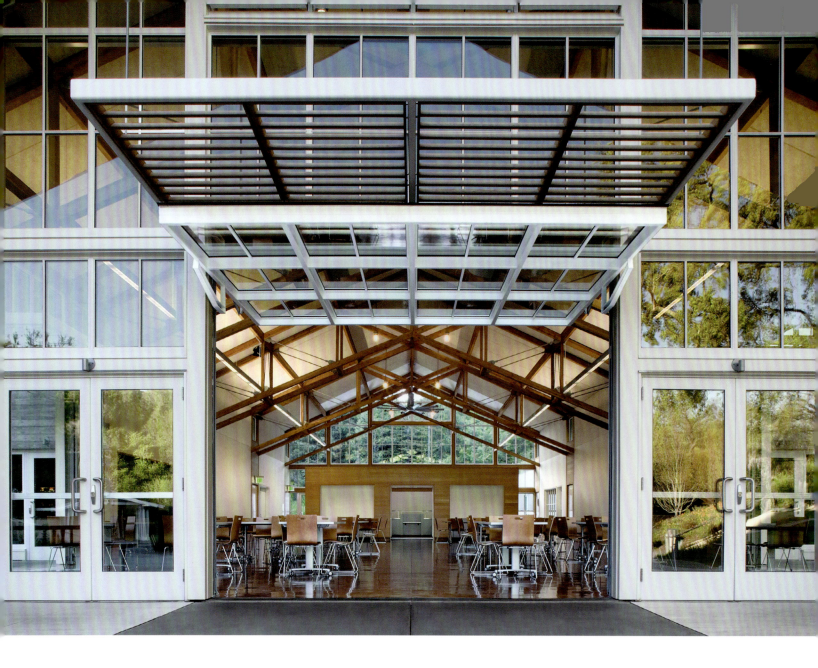

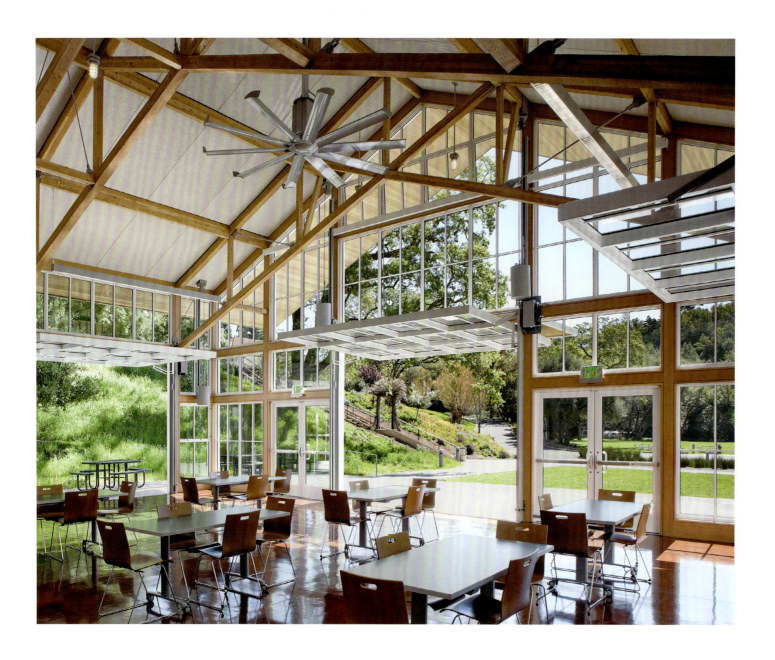

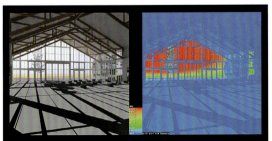
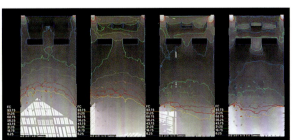
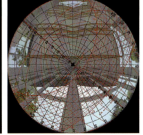

Daylight studies

145   THE COMMONS, BRANSON SCHOOL

Douglas Fine Arts Center, Branson School

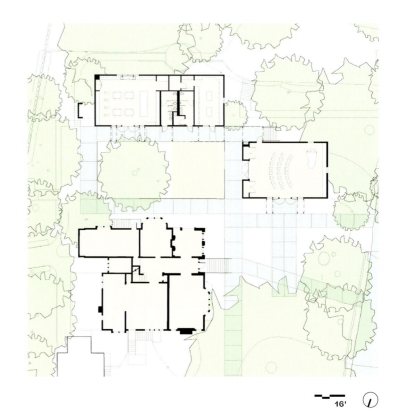

Creating a compound

The existing fine arts facilities at the Branson School occupied a former residence that had been converted into art and music studios. An overgrown side garden featured a mature oak. Our design for the Douglas Fine Arts Center divided the program into two new buildings to form a courtyard with the existing structure. The school had a fixed limit on how much new building area they could add to the campus, making outdoor spaces that opened out and connected at grade especially important. The freestanding Maxwell Music Hall features a gable roof with an entry facing the original house to create a welcoming approach to the complex. The acoustics were carefully designed in the high-ceilinged interior space. Doors fold away to connect to the courtyard, and an outdoor walkway with a translucent roof connects the music hall to a shed-roofed wing that houses digital art and sculpture studios. The new buildings are clad with cedar boards and painted to complement the original house. Given the benign climate in Ross, the art courtyard provides space for outdoor projects and classes under the shade of the oak tree.

TURNBULL GRIFFIN HAESLOOP ARCHITECTS

Hicks Mountain Ranch

*Framing a courtyard
with long views*

Sited on a gentle knoll within an expansive rural property, this 4,600-square-foot ranch house creates a gathering place for extended family and friends. Designed as a cluster of three buildings, the compound saddlebags over the hill, enclosing a wind-protected space. The outdoor courtyard with its plunge pool and hot tub mediates between the ranch's vast landscape and the interior's sheltered spaces. The shed-roofed living areas have Douglas fir walls lit by a long narrow skylight along the high side of the slope. The floors are reclaimed wood with white clapboard casework set into the wood surround. The living, dining, and cooking spaces of the main house adjoin the courtyard level, while the bedrooms and bunk rooms are tucked into a lower level that opens out to the hillside. A bridge at the entry overlooks a playroom below and opens to a large window with vistas out over the property. Carefully sited to fit onto the sloping site and harmonize with its surroundings, the compound's agrarian character is expressed by using weathered cedar siding and a corrugated zinc roof. The house is designed to be net-zero in its energy use; energy-saving solutions include a remote photovoltaic array, zoned radiant heat, sunscreens, a rainwater catchment system, and drought-tolerant landscaping. With the spectacular backdrop of the West Marin Hills, the compound frames views to the majestic Mount Tamalpais and beyond.

Salvaged logs

TURNBULL GRIFFIN HAESLOOP ARCHITECTS

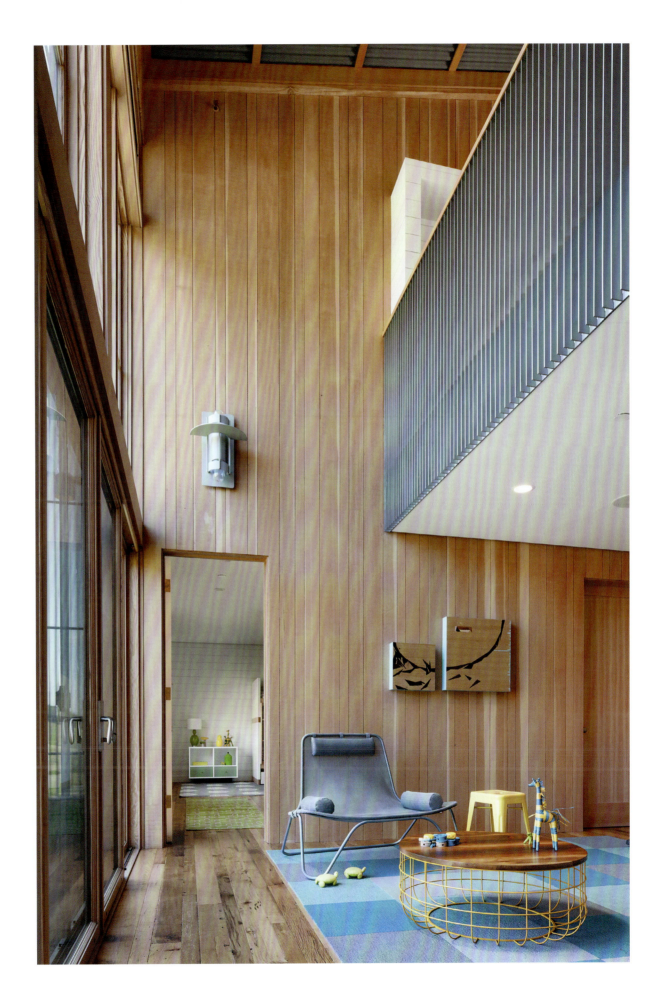

Marin Hillside

Merging with the hill

The Marin Hillside house engages the steep undulating topography of its site and captures spectacular views of San Francisco Bay and Mount Tamalpais, the highest mountain in Marin County. On our first visit, the site felt so steep that it seemed to conflict with the clients' request for a house to age in place and drive a car down to an attached garage on the same level as the primary living space. A sinuous retaining wall that follows the contours of the hill solved the challenge by anchoring the house to the site while allowing the living spaces to perch out toward the view. As you enter the house under the living roof, a glazed walkway extends between the pool courtyard and the tipped-up volumes of the living spaces. These distinct volumes are clad in reclaimed elm with shed roofs angled to catch the sun with solar collectors. They feature clerestories for natural light and ventilation from the north. On the south, a dining deck is carved in and then cantilevers along the dining/kitchen volume, opening the house to the view with large slide-away doors.

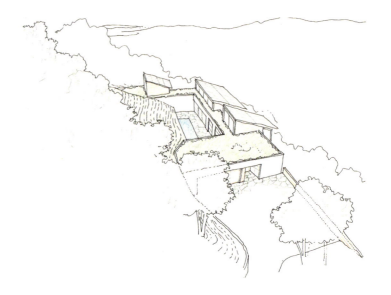

With encouragement from the clients, the form of the house incorporates many sustainable strategies as part of the architecture. The living roof collects and filters stormwater, feeding a 2,500-gallon cistern that slowly recharges back to the groundwater. The three shed roofs harvest sunlight. The high-performance windows facing out to the dramatic view feature exterior sunshades and exterior window blinds to protect the glass when needed. The residence employs a combination of passive and active cooling methodologies. With pre-cooled air drawn from the substructure crawl space and further cooled and filtered within the retaining wall, operable clerestory windows allow hot air to escape, thus circulating cool air up and throughout the house. Simple, elegant materials express the house's form. The high volumes are clad with ipe rainscreen, while a lime-based stucco envelops the remainder of the residence and connects to the concrete retaining wall, visually fusing the structure to the earthen hillside.

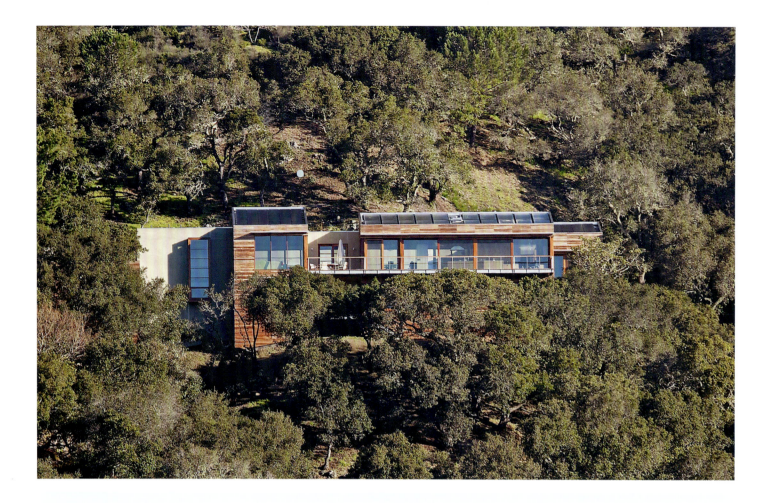

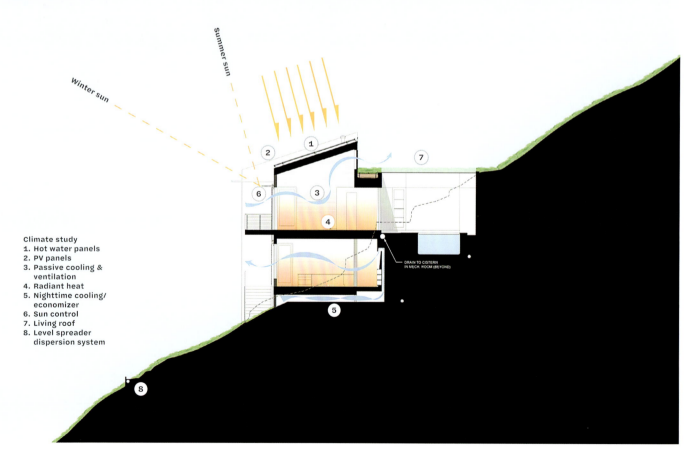

Climate study
1. Hot water panels
2. PV panels
3. Passive cooling & ventilation
4. Radiant heat
5. Nighttime cooling/ economizer
6. Sun control
7. Living roof
8. Level spreader dispersion system

TURNBULL GRIFFIN HAESLOOP ARCHITECTS

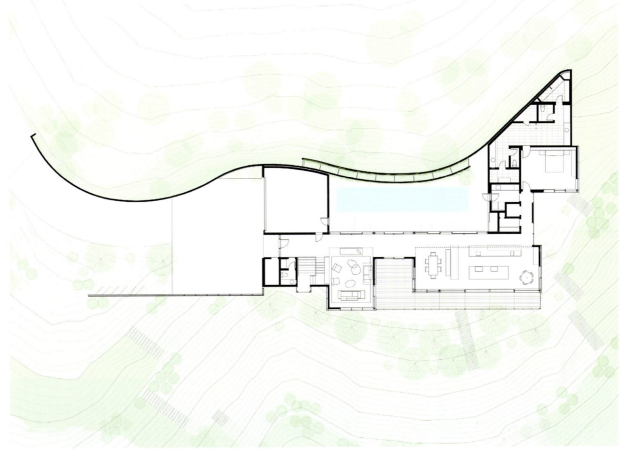

MARIN HILLSIDE

College Track San Francisco

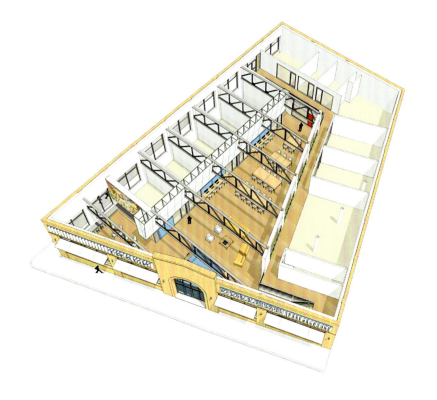

Empowering community

College Track, a nonprofit organization founded by Laurene Powell Jobs, works to empower high school students to achieve a college degree. College Track San Francisco purchased an unreinforced masonry warehouse in the Bayview neighborhood of San Francisco for a new facility to support 700 students, most of whom are from low-income households. They asked us to transform the vacant building into an engaging and welcoming center. By breathing new life into this decrepit building, located on a prominent corner site, College Track San Francisco established a strong neighborhood presence. Inside, a series of tutoring rooms cluster around a central, skylit space accented by a translucent light monitor. This is where the students and staff gather every day in a "unity circle" to reaffirm their commitment to one another and to excellence. Natural and recycled finishes complement the exposed building structure, while vibrant colors in the furnishings energize the student activity spaces. The 13,800-square-foot project includes a full seismic upgrade of the brick exterior, and the insertion of a partial second floor.

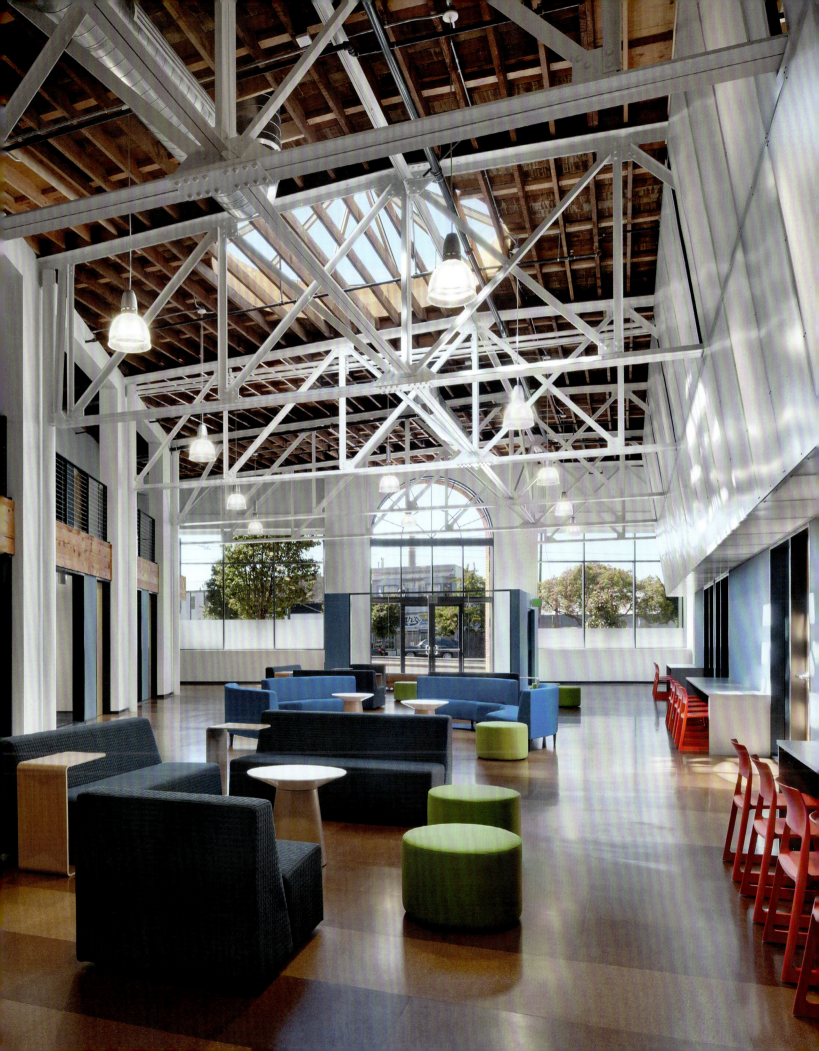

Sausalito Hillside Remodel

Perching above the bay

After purchasing a two-unit, 1940s ranch-style building that faced away from the view, collectively having a warren of small rooms, the clients requested that the units be combined to create a single-family retreat that captures the sweeping dynamic views of San Francisco Bay. Perched on a steeply sloping hillside in Sausalito, except for the garage, the house steps down the hill and is nearly invisible from the street. An elevator links the three levels of the house.

We were required to work within the footprint and height limit of the original house. The design solution removes the original aggregation of roof shapes on the upper level and creates a new flat roof that maximizes the allowable height toward the view, creating a serene, light-filled volume spanning the width of the building. A cascading series of garden terraces form an inviting entry sequence along the north side, enabling the original street-facing front yard to be developed as a private garden. Inside, floor-to-ceiling windows and generous ceiling heights allow the living spaces to flow uninterrupted from the lush backdrop of the hillside garden to the broad panorama of the bay.

The spaces are accented with the owner's beautiful art collection and Margaret Turnbull's elegant minimal interiors. The primary bedroom adjoins the great room with a slide-away door that allows for a continuous wall of floor-to-ceiling glass, looking out to the view. A balcony with a glass railing off the bedroom provides a spectacular spot to step out into the fresh air. The light-filled great room is grounded to the hillside with its carved-out garden while it reaches out to perch above the bay. The soaring sense of perching to capture the ever-changing view is balanced with a strong connection to the land.

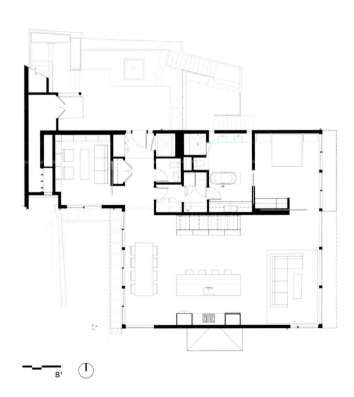

181   SAUSALITO HILLSIDE REMODEL

Coyote Camp

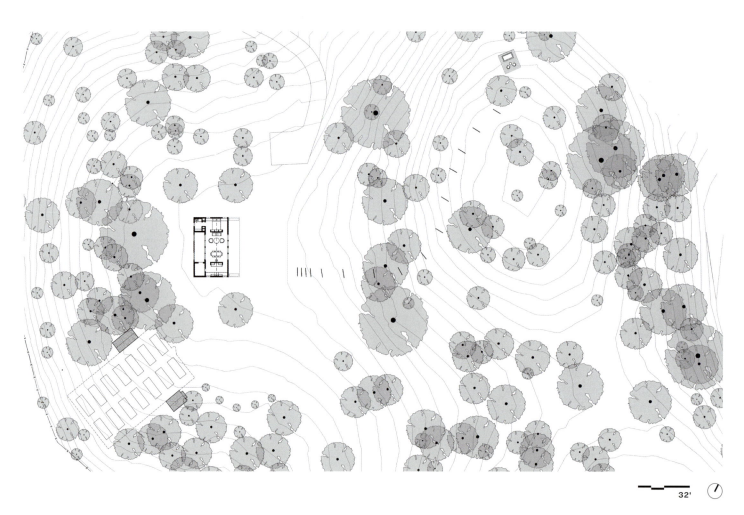

Creating a rustic retreat

Located on a remote site in Sonoma County, this 640-square-foot cabin looks like a simple barn when the sliding wooden doors are closed. Yet when the doors slide away, the house opens to both sides of the site. The one-room house centers on a living and dining area with a woodburning stove. On either side of this symmetrical space, casework screens shield the kitchen on one end and a bed inspired by Thomas Jefferson's bed at Monticello on the other end. The house's exterior consists of vertical redwood boards, milled from a reclaimed water tank, with a corrugated Corten rusted roof. The interior walls feature resawn Douglas fir with concrete floors and a floating Sheetrock ceiling. Designed to provide an indoor refuge on a site that celebrates outdoor living, the cabin serves as a gathering place to welcome family on inclement days. In addition to the cabin, the compound includes an extensive garden flanked by a bath shed and a sleeping shed. On top of the knoll, a copper soaking tub looks out to Mount Saint Helena, the landmark mountain that borders Sonoma, Napa, and Lake counties in California.

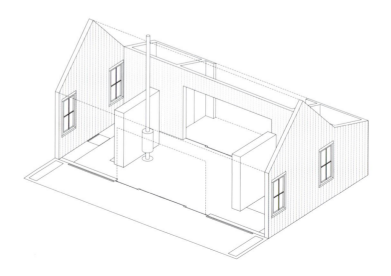

Hupomone Ranch

Barn as house typology

Hupomone Ranch consists of a 160-acre homestead located in the Chileno Valley, west of downtown Petaluma. The ranch had not been farmed for over thirty years when our clients asked us to reenvision the property as a rural compound for their extended family. Arriving, you drop down into the site from the road's higher elevation, entering a shielded valley. The white barn-shaped house claims the site and creates a threshold between the entry on the north side and the serene meadow that unfolds to the south. The symmetrically grounded form of the minimalist barn-shaped structure complements the balanced topographical quality of the valley. From the compressed entry with a loft above, you pass into the high-ceilinged great room with a fully glazed end wall, that looks out to the meadow and beyond to long views to the coastal range. The great room is shaped by a high gable ceiling that folds down to the kitchen. The floating stairs and loft above create scale and spatial complexity. The room is luminous with natural light, and a skylight washes the north wall and balances the full glazing of the south wall with its overhanging roof. The main house bedrooms and kitchen occupy the lower saddlebag wings of the barn to either side. The kitchen features slide-away windows that open directly to the vegetable garden. The meadow and house are centered on the valley floor and a series of outdoor spaces, including the garden, firepit, and outdoor dining area terrace along the eastern side of the meadow, culminate in the pool and pool house. The project is certified LEED Platinum and includes such sustainable features as geothermal, radiant cooling and heating and photovoltaic panels. With the support of committed owners, the design of the new compound reclaims and restores the site.

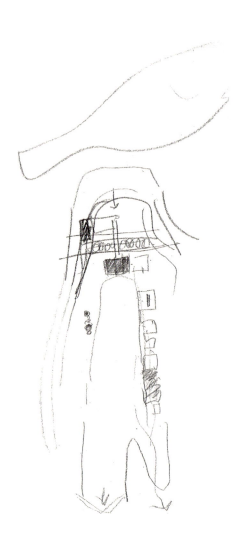

TURNBULL GRIFFIN HAESLOOP ARCHITECTS

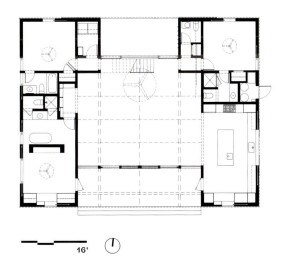

201 HUPOMONE RANCH

Cloverdale Vineyard

Reclaiming the site

Located above Cloverdale on a steep hill overlooking vineyards and the valley below, this house replaces an uninsulated log kit house that occupied the only flat area of the site. While wanting to preserve the mature oak trees, the pool, and the access drives, the client suggested we salvage and mill the logs from the existing structure to reuse in a sustainable, energy-efficient house. With the intention to minimally impact the site, our design reorients a new house on the existing footprint to overlook the pool and claim expansive views over the vineyards to the south.

The client's memories of growing up with wrap-around screened porches in a house designed by William Turnbull Jr. inspired us to design a large screened porch. A folding glass wall between the dining area and the porch allows for flexible indoor/outdoor living and the option of one continuous space under the sloped roof. The porch becomes an integral part of the house and a circulation link to the guest bedrooms as well as to the deck and pool below.

The shape of the house is two parallel volumes. Support spaces are located on the entry side under a flat living roof that links the volume to the grassy hill above. A parallel shed-roofed form contains the primary spaces opening to the larger landscape. The roof tips up to the north with a band of clerestory windows, allowing soft light to enter the main living spaces and balance the direct light of the south-facing windows that are protected with exterior sunscreens. The slope of the roof accommodates solar panels.

The corrugated Corten exterior cladding addresses both wildfire and maintenance concerns. The interior and exterior wood paneling, trim, and decking were milled from the logs of the original kit house. The house is passively cooled with solar-powered heat pumps, providing either radiant heating or cooling depending on seasonal needs. Through careful rethinking, the new house claims the special features of the site and reflects the clients' commitment to sustainability.

TURNBULL GRIFFIN HAESLOOP ARCHITECTS

Berkeley Cottage

Shaping the garden

Located in a densely developed neighborhood near the UC Berkeley campus, surrounded by transit lines and a small commercial district, the Berkeley Cottage provides much needed car-free rental housing. We designed the new, 430-square-foot accessory dwelling unit to reshape and enhance an existing backyard, providing privacy and protecting views for both the new cottage and the existing house.

The main house, built in 1908, sits near the front of the 50 by 140-foot lot, with mature trees flanking the edges. By removing an old garage and driveway that had dominated the rear garden, the new cottage was sited across the back of the deep lot. The design solution shapes the garden by creating a gabled structure that edges the rear line of the property. By concentrating the fenestration on either end of the gable, views out are focused into greenery and keep the unit secluded from neighbors, which also preserves the privacy of the main house's garden. The cottage's vine wall visually reinforces the garden's edge.

The cottage is built with structurally insulated panels, which provide a continuously insulated shell and span the length of the roof, allowing for a clean expression of the gable on the inside. Within the space, a block containing the bath, kitchen, and storage area is located near the center, creating separation and privacy between the sleeping and living areas. The white Sheetrock walls and ceiling with a flush skylight and east-facing windows introduce natural light throughout the day. The floors are reclaimed valley oak. This structure illustrates how to create both housing and an improved backyard by favoring people over cars. With good design and careful manipulation of light and space, a small structure becomes an inviting retreat.

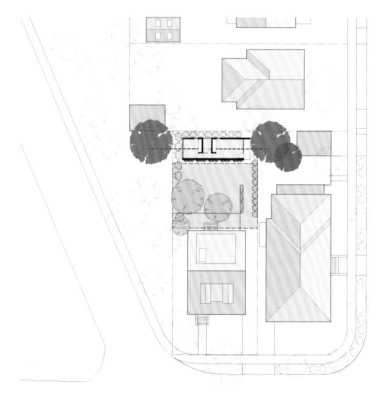

Prefab panels

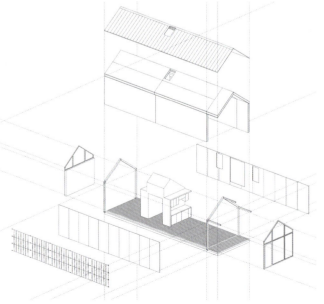

Assembly diagram

Sonoma Retreat

Framing the pond

The site, a meadow scattered with magnificent oaks, gently slopes down to a spring-fed pond, creating an unusually lush landscape in arid Sonoma County. The owners requested that the house be designed for indoor/outdoor living. They wanted guests to arrive and have easy access to the pool and pond beyond without entering the main house. This compound of buildings brackets a verdant oak meadow, loosely defining a space within the larger landscape. Stepping down from the car court, a thin floating roof supported by a concrete cooking fireplace reaches across the outdoor living space to create a dramatic threshold to the lawn and pond beyond. The adjoining indoor living/dining space, also located under the high roof, features clerestory windows on all sides and a window wall facing toward the pond. Exposed Douglas fir framing defines a screen wall that wraps under the clerestory to create a warm filigree. A second freestanding concrete element completes the roof structure and houses the woodstove and bookcases. The bedrooms, kitchen, and support spaces are located under a living roof that visually links the house to the surrounding landscape. The pool house extends the outdoor living with generous shade trellises cantilevered over the pool. The structure includes a playroom, changing room, and guest room. At the pond's edge, a firepit and small dock create another destination.

Designed to be net-zero in its energy usage, the residence includes passive cooling strategies such as a cool roof, a living roof, high R-value insulation, operable windows, and large overhangs, allowing the interior to remain comfortable without air-conditioning. The house merges with the landscape to create finely tuned indoor and outdoor spaces for living on this distinctive site.

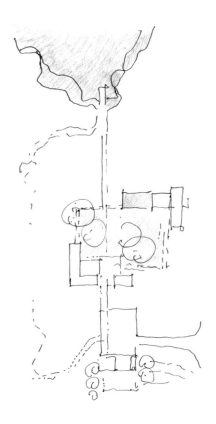

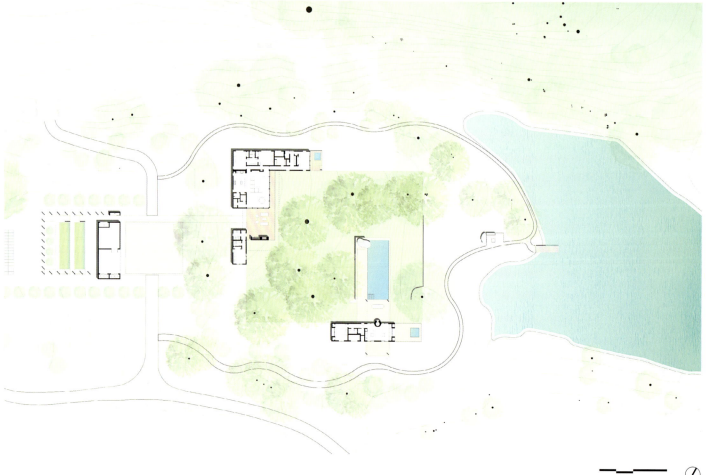

SONOMA RETREAT

TURNBULL GRIFFIN HAESLOOP ARCHITECTS

Stinson Beach Lagoon

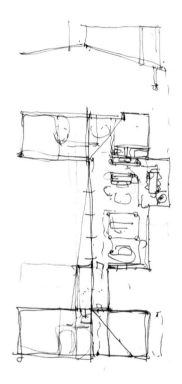

Reaching to the views

Located at Stinson Beach, this site opens directly onto the south side of the Seadrift Lagoon and looks north to the Bolinas Lagoon and the Marin Hills. This house, built on a double lot, creates an indoor/outdoor retreat to share with extended family and friends. From the quiet access road, as you arrive at the front door, you see through a compressed entry to the porch, with decks stepping down to a dock on the lagoon. The building form is a butterfly roof carved away to form a courtyard to the south. The courtyard captures the sun and blocks the wind while also providing privacy for the deck, firepit, and hot tub. The living spaces flow outdoors to the porch and courtyard. The dining bay, on the opposite side of the space, reaches up to the north to capture views of the Bolinas Lagoon and the hills beyond. Designed for a family of cooks, the kitchen is central and generous, surrounded with choices for reading in a window seat, around the fireplace, or out on the deck.

Two primary bedroom suites are located on one side of the living spaces and two bunk rooms on the other. We designed the interior of the house to feature the owners' art collection with white Sheetrock walls sized for specific pieces. The cedar board interior ceiling, with a crisp fold at the low point of the butterfly, connects the indoors to the surroundings. The floors are wide-board oak, and the exterior is untreated vertical cedar boards with metal windows and doors. The house becomes a refuge between inviting outdoor activities and peaceful views of the ever-changing lagoons.

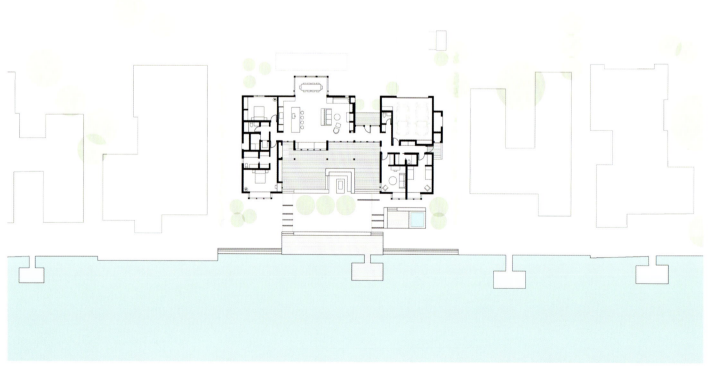

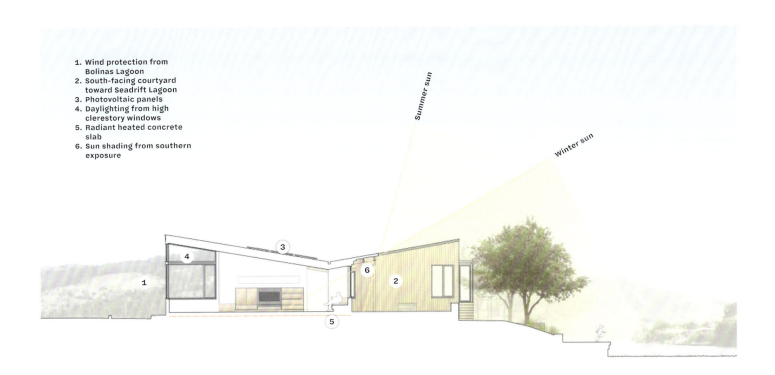

1. Wind protection from Bolinas Lagoon
2. South-facing courtyard toward Seadrift Lagoon
3. Photovoltaic panels
4. Daylighting from high clerestory windows
5. Radiant heated concrete slab
6. Sun shading from southern exposure

Portola Valley Garden

Circling the garden

This Portola Valley compound features two gabled pavilions linked by a low wing with a living roof. Backing onto open space, the site faces out to long views of the coastal hills. The clients are creative artists and makers, and they requested a series of spaces to pursue their varied interests; her studio includes a loom and drafting board, and his features movable tables for building computers, speakers, and prototypes. Their wish list included a wood workshop as well. She is also a master gardener and dreamed of an unfenced native garden, with a special space for succulents, where she could continually experiment with plants. In addition, they have an extensive art collection and desired spaces to display paintings.

Our design creates a compound of linked buildings attuned to the clients' program, the site, and its views. An entry car court is edged by the gabled workshop adjoining the low carport wing with a living roof. This building stretches to the high gabled main pavilion, canted to face the view. The compound surrounds an entry garden that centers on a stone circle featuring the clients' succulent collection. The front door brings you into the high space that encloses all the living functions of the house. The gable roof extends to become a porch that looks out to the distant hills and creates shade for the fully glazed window wall and the outdoor living space. A floating stair connects to an overlook and the primary bedroom, with a private deck looking over open space to San Francisco Bay. In the low wing, the linked studios feature slide-away doors opening to outdoor workspaces. The walkway that leads along the studios to the carport is edged by a long bookcase that displays the clients' extensive library.

The exterior walls are unfinished cedar, the gable roofs are zinc, and the flat living roofs filter rainwater into a 10,000-gallon cistern used for irrigating the garden. Sliding sunshades allow the clients to customize the house's temperature and adjust the sun exposure in the main living areas and workshop. We were inspired by the unusual program to create a set of forms and spaces responding to the site and the clients' varied interests.

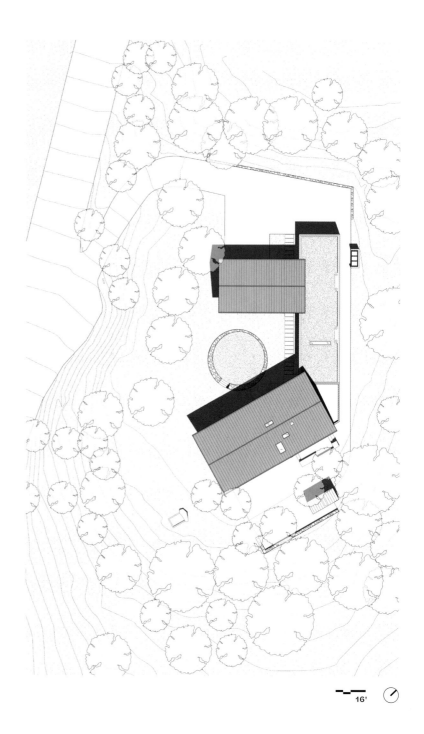

Climate and rainwater
1. 10,000-gallon rainwater catchment system for garden
2. Low-velocity ceiling fan for whole house; no A/C
3. Closed cell insulation for entire building envelope
4. Sliding adjustable sunscreens
5. Living roof
6. Garden with succulents and native plants; no fencing

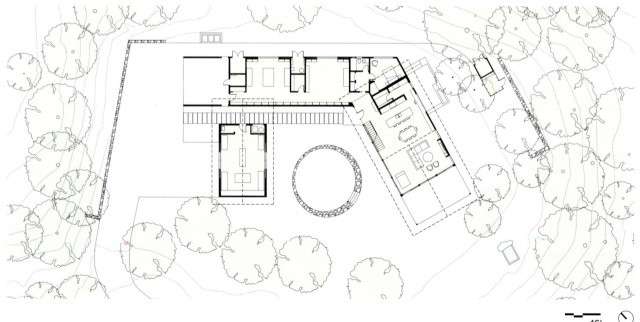

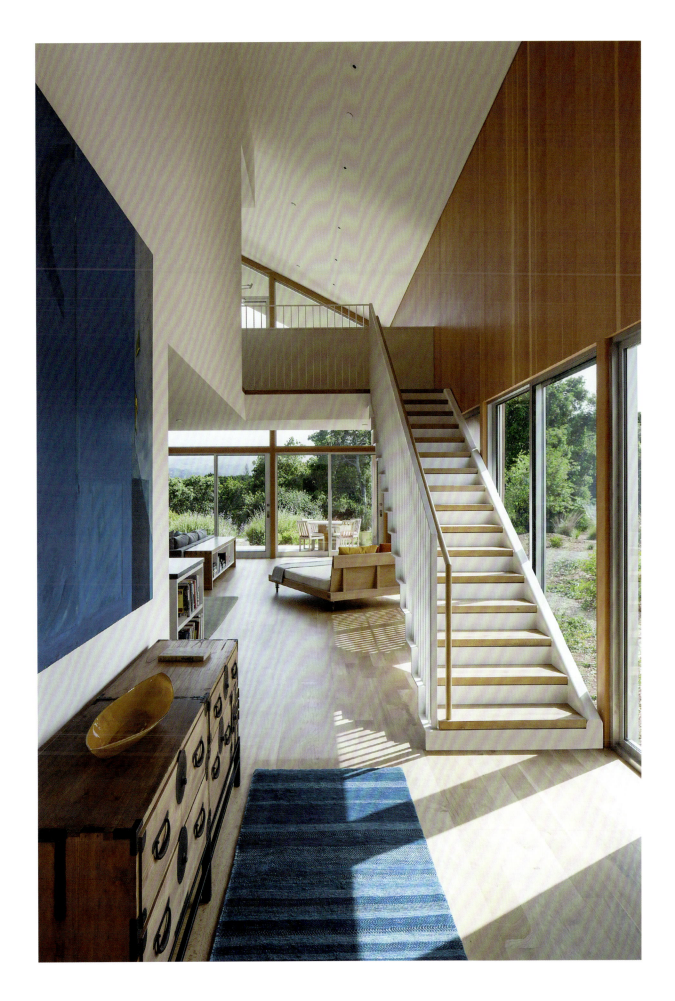

PORTOLA VALLEY GARDEN

Skyfall, The Sea Ranch

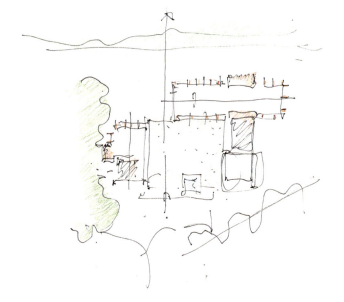

Overlooking the fairway

Skyfall creatively explores an alternative way of building at The Sea Ranch in the era of climate change and when wood has become precious and vulnerable. The house occupies a unique setting on a cul-de-sac bordered by golf links. A large stand of cypress trees anchors the southern edge of the site, while to the north and west broad views sweep across the fairways to the Pacific Ocean, bluff-front houses, and clusters of trees along the Gualala River.

Our response to the site and the clients' program creates simple barnlike forms that nestle against the cypress stand to shape a courtyard that screens the golf course and the wind. The entry gate of the compound frames a view between the two buildings across the fairway to the Pacific Ocean, while the courtyard functions as the center of the house.

The long gable roof houses the study/living/kitchen/dining spaces with a syncopated window wall that stretches the length of the space, following the sweep of the fairway. A protected window seat punctuates the window wall, creating an intimate space across from the kitchen island within the larger volume. The guest room tower forms the north side of the courtyard with solar panels set below the parapet. The primary bedroom is in a detached structure anchoring the courtyard.

The clients requested exploring fire-safe materials that require minimal maintenance and age well. The early Sea Ranch barns and buildings featured wood on both roofs and walls; we looked for an alternative material that would honor this original design intent and chose cement panels to clad both the walls and the roof. The ribbed texture of the cement panels softens the material's appearance and settles the house into the landscape. Wood is used sparingly in places that one experiences close at hand, such as the windows and the entry porch. Structural wood fins articulate the window wall as in exposed barn framing.

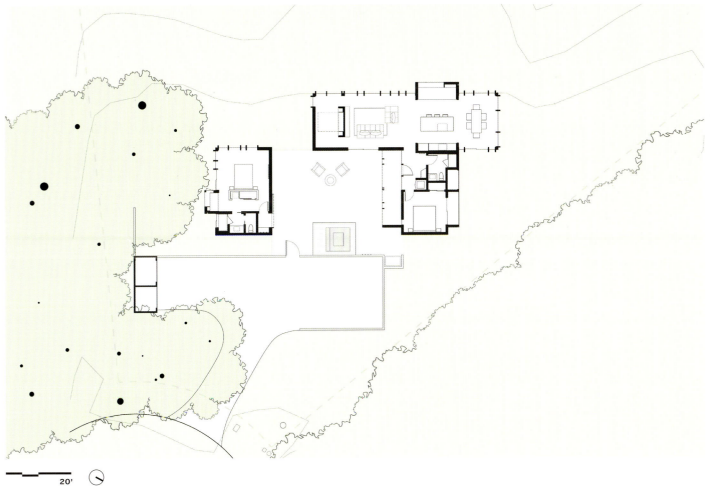

20'

Carmel Valley Retreat

Terracing the hill with earth walls

Located in the Santa Lucia Preserve in Carmel Valley, the twenty-two-acre site drops downhill to a gently sloping expansive meadow anchored by a grove of oaks to the east with a broad view to the south. When visiting another Turnbull Griffin Haesloop house designed with sprayed earth walls, our clients responded to the warmth and texture of the material and requested we include the material in the design of their Carmel Valley house. Sprayed earth walls organize the site, creating terraces that extend and merge into the landscape, setting up buildable zones for a linear compound of buildings—house, guesthouse, garage, and accessory dwelling unit, as well as outdoor spaces. On the entry court side, the earth walls merge into the hill, enclosing the garage, while a high wall on the main house creates separation from cars. On either side of the front door, two earth cubes flank a hallway leading into the airy glass-walled living and dining space, articulated with a delicate wood structure.

Linked by a walkway and edged by sprayed-earth site walls leading to the entry, the guesthouse further explores combinations of sprayed earth and exposed wood construction. The rough walls on the north side read through to the interior but are held down for clerestory windows. The roof butterflies up in both directions to capture the light and views.

The accessory dwelling unit sits farther up the hill. Sprayed earth walls retain the grade, creating an inset protected courtyard lined by *shou sugi ban* wooden walls. On the interior, light plays between white Sheetrock, black exterior siding, oak casework, and sprayed earth. The loosely linked compound of buildings sits quietly among the terraced walls, each building gesturing to its unique site and program.

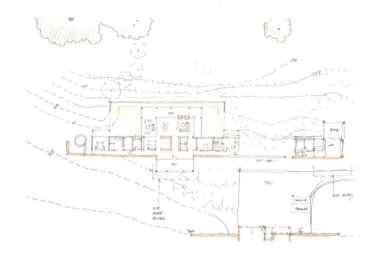

TURNBULL GRIFFIN HAESLOOP ARCHITECTS

CARMEL VALLEY RETREAT

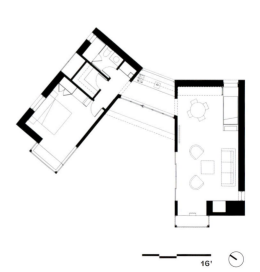

TURNBULL GRIFFIN HAESLOOP ARCHITECTS

CARMEL VALLEY RETREAT

Healdsburg Knoll

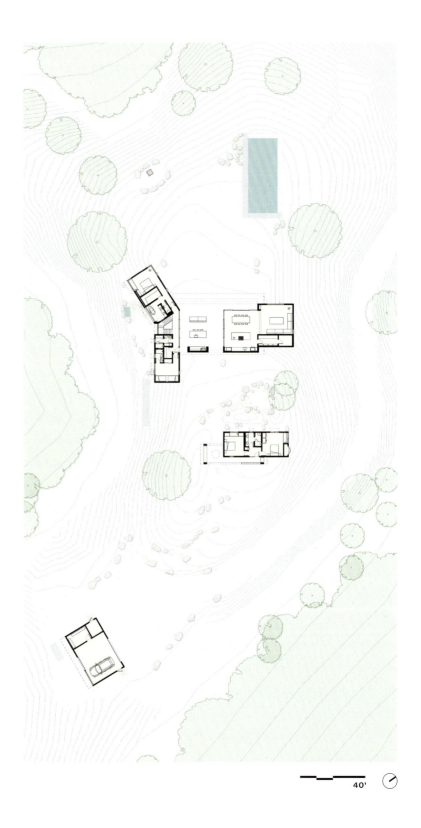

Draping the knoll

Located in a remote area of Sonoma County, Healdsburg Knoll is sited on a large tract of sharply sloping land with many different features, including oak meadows and steep canyons. The owners requested that the design of the new compound incorporate their desire to live outdoors as much as indoors. Visiting the site together, we were all drawn to a distinctive landform about halfway up the hill—a knoll on a promontory that folded down into a peninsula below with sweeping views out to vineyards and distant hills. In choosing to build on this special site, we wanted to preserve the legibility of the landform. The owners were also interested in creating a sense of procession from the entry point up and over the knoll. We separated the program pieces, siting the guesthouse upon the knoll. A square porch with a circular opening marks the entry into the compound.

You then walk down an axial path, passing a sculptural concrete cooking fireplace that anchors the outdoor living room. The pavilion roof floats above the outdoor living area and the indoor kitchen/dining space, creating a shaded retreat from the summer sun and gesturing out to the lawn, pool, and broad landscape beyond. On either side of the glassy high pavilion, Corten-clad wings settle the house into the landscape. Following the topography, the southern bedroom wing cants out to gesture to the lower peninsula. A dramatic stair connects down to the lower-level bedrooms and terrace. The other wing drapes down the contour of the knoll to enclose the indoor living space. A minimalist swimming pool with infinity edges on two sides creates a reflecting pool at the far edge of the lawn.

The Healdsburg Knoll project was just beginning construction in fall 2019 when a massive wildfire burned through the site, destroying majestic oak trees and pine forests. Construction resumed but the design of the project was modified to harden the exterior materials and site infrastructure to resist wildfires. Additional water storage tanks were added, and the proposed wood siding was replaced with Corten steel panels, reflecting the best building practices after a forest fire and hopefully providing a magical retreat for many decades to come.

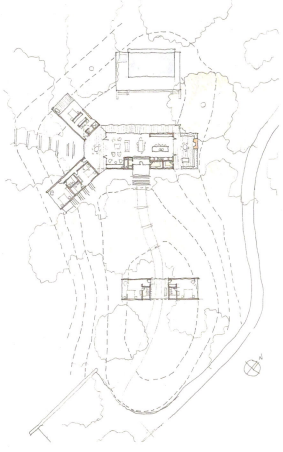

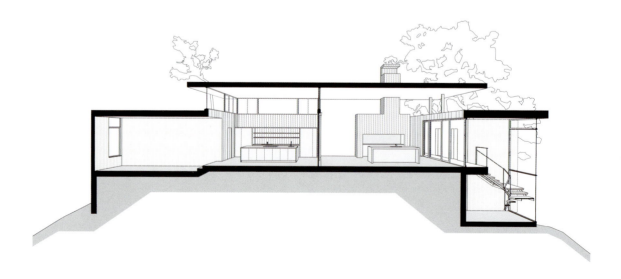

TURNBULL GRIFFIN HAESLOOP ARCHITECTS

Paths

Mary Griffin

I was born in Atlanta, Georgia, in the same year that my parents completed construction on a butterfly-roof house on the edge of the campus of Emory University, where my father was a professor. It was designed by Paul Heffernan, who had studied at Harvard's Graduate School of Design before joining the Georgia Tech architecture faculty, where he remained for thirty-five years. He was a modern architect influenced by Walter Gropius, and my father had met him when they both taught at Georgia Tech during World War II. The Griffin house was one of the few residences he designed, and it suggested a very modern way to live on a suburban lot. The house was sited tight to the northwest corner, and the southern exposure, where the roof tipped up, was a glazed wall opening onto a large side garden. The house had an open plan circling around a central block composed of closets and high bookcases that did not go up to the ceiling, creating a perfect aerie for children to nest in. The house was modest, but it was magical.

My father was a sociologist involved in the civil rights movement and equity in education, not an architect. But he loved light and patterns and architecture. As a child growing up in the house, I was enthralled with the mystery of space and light. I remember suggesting to my younger brother that he become an architect. In Atlanta in the 1950s there were no women architects and I perceived architecture as a field reserved for men. Early memories of hiding from the Georgia Tech architecture students coming to tour the house, all young men, reinforced this belief.

At seventeen, I went off to Brown University, at my father's urging, leaving the South for my college years. I never returned. I was a liberal arts student studying history and literature. It was 1969, and everything was changing. We protested against the Vietnam War and demonstrated for women's rights. In a modern architectural history course taught by William Jordy I became fascinated by the links he made between history and buildings as expressions of culture. In a seminar with Jordy the next year, I did a presentation on public housing, and I discovered articles by John Zeisel, an architectural sociologist at the Harvard Graduate School of Design, studying how people

experienced architecture. I met Zeisel at Harvard and he agreed to advise my honor's thesis with Jordy and invited me to audit a class he was teaching at the GSD comparing the architect's intentions and residents' perceptions in affordable housing, trying to incorporate a feedback loop into the design of housing based on what residents experienced. I concurrently conducted my own study in Providence, Rhode Island, of Mount Hope Courts, interviewing William Warner, the architect of the infill housing project, and the residents of the development, using questionnaires and in-person visits. It was fascinating to see the bridge between the world of architectural design and the lives of those in affordable housing. The housing units were simple duplexes with pitched roofs and wood siding designed to infill into a typical New England wood-frame neighborhood. But the architect decided to leave the cedar siding natural and let it age like The Sea Ranch Condominium 1 had exemplified to the world. One of the residents commented that it was too bad the developers could not afford paint—to anyone from the South unpainted buildings were a sign of poverty, not architectural innovation. Little did I know that The Sea Ranch Condominium 1 (and its designers), which Jordy had shown in the last lecture of his modern architecture class, would come to play such a significant role in my own life.

After graduating from Brown in 1973, I moved to Cambridge to work with Zeisel in the architectural research office at Harvard. We conducted post-occupancy evaluations of housing projects and research into how the design of school buildings might discourage vandalism.

Not sure of the next step on my path, I considered becoming a planner or a sociologist, but I loved design. Harvard allowed employees to take a summer class and I chose a three-dimensional design class taught by Lou Bakanowsky, the chair of Harvard's Visual and Environmental Studies department, housed in Le Corbusier's Carpenter Center. At the end of the course, which included designing a house, Lou said to me, "Mary, you should become an architect." That was the push I needed to apply to architecture school. In the fall of 1975, I enrolled at MIT, where Donlyn Lyndon was just stepping down as chair of the Architecture department. The next chapter of my life began.

At MIT, I studied with Jan Wampler and Maurice Smith, where the focus was on experiential architecture and ways of making. More significantly, in the fall of 1977, I studied at the International Laboratory of Architecture and Urban Design in Urbino, Italy. Under Giancarlo De Carlo and Donlyn Lyndon's guiding humanistic vision, students from seven countries collaborated on projects and experienced the beauty and awe of living in Urbino and Rome. After returning to MIT, Donlyn was my mentor—he advised my thesis and together we designed my first built house. My aunt and uncle in Starkville, Mississippi, were the clients.

After moving to Washington, DC, I practiced for five years with Hartman-Cox Architects, working with George Hartman on the design and construction of a fascinating array of projects, always carefully rooted in their contexts. My life took an unexpected turn when Donlyn visited Washington for an awards jury and invited me to join his fellow jurors Charles Moore and Bill Turnbull for dinner. A year later, in 1985, I moved to San Francisco to marry Bill. I joined his firm, bringing my interest in small institutional projects and how people inhabit and perceive space. With Bill I learned to appreciate and to read the California landscapes. A brilliant designer, Bill was a master at siting buildings. Our collaboration, guided by our intention to design buildings that enhance their settings and their clients' lives, is illustrated in our small house at Teviot Springs Vineyard and at St. Andrew's Presbyterian Church in Sonoma, both National AIA Honor Award projects.

Bill struggled valiantly with cancer for seven years and died in 1997. I was forty-five with two young sons. With Eric Haesloop's support, I decided to continue the firm and transition it from William Turnbull Associates to Turnbull Griffin Haesloop. This monograph shares the work that Eric and I have designed together with our talented collaborators and consultants. We have been committed to honoring Bill's legacy while finding our own voice as we responded to a changing world.

Eric Haesloop

My path to becoming an architect started long before I had any idea what architecture might be or could encompass. Like many first-generation children of immigrants, I grew up in two cultures. My parents emigrated from Germany immediately after World War II. The open landscape of the United States, their newly adopted home country, felt liberating. Indiana's expanses of farmland and extensive deciduous forests became home. I often joined them when they went back to Germany to travel and visit my grandparents, developing a connection to a rich tradition of European art and architecture.

I entered the undergraduate program in the School of Architecture at Washington University in St. Louis in 1974 specifically because it was set within a liberal arts framework, ideal for exploring different areas of study. I sketched the vernacular architecture of St. Louis and the agricultural buildings stretching across the Midwest. I took semesters abroad at the University of Salamanca in Spain and at the University of Tübingen in Germany. In Tübingen, I participated in a seminar on the architectural manifestos of the early twentieth century, which bridged the theoretical and tangible. We read the visionary philosophies of seminal architects and planners, such as Le Corbusier and Ludwig Mies van der Rohe. We then visited and experienced buildings in the nearby Weissenhof Estate in Stuttgart, Germany.

The graduate program at the Yale School of Architecture offered so much to me, including the first-year building project; Vincent Scully for architectural history; Alec Purves for surveying precedents; Charles Moore for understanding the importance of delight in architecture; James Stirling for grasping the importance of layering diagrams to develop a design rich with human experience; and Aldo Rossi for an exploration of typologies. In the summers I worked for an architect in Zug, Switzerland, where my in-laws lived. In my last year at Yale, I started working for César Pelli, whose office was just down the block from the Yale Art + Architecture Building. Working at César Pelli and Associates for three years after graduation, I learned how César's designs took shape by studying options, often with physical models, through progressive iterations.

I joined William Turnbull Associates a few years after graduate school and felt like I had found my architectural home. One of the first projects I worked on with Bill was the Spencer Residence in Napa Valley. The project was ordered but adjusted to the site, an interpretation of Napa's vernacular architecture but thoroughly modern in its use of space and light. Later designs brought Bill's use of space and light to a wide range of projects in different settings, always drawing inspiration from the context of landscape. For the Sandler Apartment, located in a high-rise tower on Russian Hill in San Francisco we looked to the curved shoreline and views below to organize the plan and give the walls their sinuous shape. In the case of the Long Meadow Ranch in St. Helena, we went a step further, not only siting the winery and olive oil press to work with the hillside but also building the walls with earth from the site and cave excavations.

Bill was an amazing teacher by example. During my twelve years designing with Bill, I worked with him to craft buildings that shaped space, framed views, and enhanced the experience of living on the land.

Working at William Turnbull Associates synthesized many of my early architectural explorations. After Bill's death in 1997, Mary and I decided to form Turnbull Griffin Haesloop. Our challenge was to complete ongoing projects such as Long Meadow Ranch and to reimagine the practice. Bill's longtime business partner Robert Simpson was instrumental in helping us transition the firm and guided us in the challenges of running a small design practice so that it would continue to be an engaging place to work and explore design. With new clients came new opportunities, along with the need to follow evolving building codes and address the changing climate. Our designs over the last twenty-eight years show how we at TGH innovated and refined our approach, to both site and buildings, while always aiming to create designs that enhance their settings and enrich the lives of the people who inhabit them.

Margaret Turnbull

Growing up in a family that relished the rural environment, architecture, art, and "modern" (now "midcentury") design most certainly influenced the choices I've made and allowed much serendipity into my life. My childhood was spent on a working East Coast farm, surrounded by cattle, sheep, horses, chickens, dogs, and cats, enjoying the distinct changing of seasons in an idyllic, insulated valley with a trout stream meandering through it. From my earliest memories, I had a rich sense of place and of being a tiny piece in a much greater landscape.

After the visceral education of childhood, my formal education focusing on studio art, art history, and education, and then a "working" graduate school managing the display for four Design Research (D/R) stores on the West Coast, I had the privilege of being invited to join William Turnbull Associates, which subsequently became Turnbull Griffin Haesloop Architects, as their interior designer. My charge as part of the team was to sometimes guide, and always accompany, the client—to be able to make choices to best complement the architectural project's overall integrity.

The layering of floor plans, finishes, colors, textures, and, crucially, the scale of the furnishings sought to reference the landscape in which the project was built. The hope and intent was to begin a process for the clients to continue this layering as travels and life progressed. Our interiors were meant to "prime the pump" and encourage sensitivity to the total environment.

People

Principals
Mary Griffin
Eric Haesloop
Stefan Hastrup

Interior Designer
Margaret Turnbull

Associates
Matt Au
Jerome Christensen
Sara Dewey
Mark Hoffman
Emily Huang
Yan Huang
John Kleman
Andrew Mann
Evan Markiewicz
Susi Marzuola
Jule Tsai
Michael Yoshida

Team
Stephanie Choo
Marina Christodoulides
John Clarke
Sean Culman
Charles Davis
Nancy DeBruyn
Andrej Dekleva
Allison Dutoit
Sydnor Elkins
Peggy Frederic
June Goodyear
Mayumi Hara
Juliet Hsu
A. L. Hu
Alexandra Jones
Kevin Killen
Arley Kim
Georgianna Salz Kleman
John Klopf
Brian Lang
Jacqueline Lin
Molly McGrath
Nancy Mei
Andrew Miller
Maya Missana
Dave Monk
Balz Mueller
Fernando Nocedal
Diepriye Olali
Ceara O'Leary
Nicholas Papaefthimiou
Steve Phillips
Edward Rendle
Alice Roche
Saand
Anne-Katrin Schulz
Colin Searles
Andrea Sessa
Chris Shelton
Timothy Sloat
Ryan Stahlman
Madeline Stokoe
Andrew Stolz
Gene Templeton
Andrew Turnbull
Matthew Waxman
Lawson Willard
Tory Wolcott
Ege Yener

Chronology

1997 Beach Studio* The Sea Ranch

1998 St. Francis Wood Remodel San Francisco
Long Meadow Ranch Guesthouse* St. Helena
Elmwood Remodel Berkeley
Long Meadow Ranch Winery and Olive Oil Press* St. Helena
Mill Valley Public Library*
Knoll Top Residence* Napa

1999 Hillside Residence* Napa County
Noe Valley Residence San Francisco
The San Francisco School
Private Residence Pebble Beach

2000 Private Residence St. Helena
Nueva School Gym Hillsborough

2001 Skjerven Morrill LLP Office San Francisco

2002 Garden Residence The Sea Ranch

2003 Bluff Trail Residence The Sea Ranch
Sausalito Remodel
Oceanfront Residence Stinson Beach
Private Residence Nicasio
St. Hilary School Tiburon
The Hamlin School San Francisco

2004 Connor Creek Ranch Colorado
Private Residence Mendocino County
Bluff Residence The Sea Ranch
Cougar Cottage Inverness

2005 CDSP Master Plan Berkeley

2006 CDSP Easton Hall Berkeley
MLTW Remodel The Sea Ranch
Redhawk Vineyard Addition Pope Valley

2007 Residence Santa Lucia Preserve
Sandler Foundation San Francisco
Lake Tahoe Retreat Nevada

2008 Sebastopol Camp
Atherton Retreat
Grace Magil Arts and Science Building,
    Burke's School San Francisco
Meadow I The Sea Ranch
Library Remodel, Burke's School San Francisco

2009 Douglas Fine Arts Center, Branson School Ross
The Commons, Branson School Ross

2010 Hicks Mountain Ranch Marin County
Marin Hillside Residence Kentfield

2011 Tomales Bay Remodel Inverness

2012 College Track San Francisco
Hillside Remodel Sausalito
Coyote Camp Calistoga

2013 College Track Los Angeles
Hupomone Ranch Petaluma
Stevenson School Faculty Housing 1 Pebble Beach
Vineyard Residence Cloverdale

2014 Berkeley Cottage Berkeley
Guesthouse Mendocino County
Grace Cathedral Kitchen Remodel San Francisco
Burke's Lower School Remodel San Francisco
Sonoma Retreat Sonoma County

2015 Guesthouse Mill Valley
Lagoon Residence Stinson Beach
Larkin Street Youth Center San Francisco

2017 Portola Valley Garden Residence
Rush House Additions The Sea Ranch
St. John's Episcopal Church Lobby Montclair
Napa Hillside Residence Napa Valley

2018 Skyfall Residence The Sea Ranch
Private Residence Mill Valley
Ella Hill Hutch Community Center San Francisco
LMR Rutherford Estate Winery Rutherford (unbuilt)
Stevenson School Faculty Housing 2 Pebble Beach

2019 Kenwood Residence Sonoma County
Sonoma Mountain Remodel Sonoma County
LMR Offices St. Helena

2020 Farmstead Lodging at LMR St. Helena (unbuilt)
Emerald Hills Residence San Mateo
Knights Valley Residence Calistoga

2021 Meadow II The Sea Ranch
C. Mayhew Remodel Piedmont

2023 Carmel Valley Retreat

2024 Healdsburg Knoll Sonoma County

*Projects started with William Turnbull

Credits

Stinson Beach Oceanfront House
Architect Turnbull Griffin Haesloop
Landscape Architect Mae Arbegast, and Las Baulinas Nursery
Interior Stylist Margaret Turnbull
Structural Fratessa Forbes Wong
Energy BEC Associates
Contractor Cove Construction

Sausalito Remodel
Architect Turnbull Griffin Haesloop
Landscape Architect Lutsko Associates, DELA
Interiors Turnbull Griffin Haesloop
Structural Richard Hartwell, MKM Associates
Contractor David Adams

Connor Creek Ranch
Architect Turnbull Griffin Haesloop
Colorado, Construction Admin Lisa Egger, Architect
Landscape Architect Winston Associates
Interior Stylist Maragaret Turnbull
Structural JVA Incorporated
Energy Mountain Parks Electric
Contractor Byron Miller Construction

Sea Ranch Bluff
Architect Turnbull Griffin Haesloop
Interiors Turnbull Griffin Haesloop
Structural Fratessa Forbes Wong
Energy BEC Associates
Contractor Timothy Carpenter

Santa Lucia Preserve
Architect Turnbull Griffin Haesloop
Landscape Architect Joni L. Janecki & Associates
Landscape Consultant Michelle Comeau
Interiors Turnbull Griffin Haesloop
Structural Fratessa Forbes Wong
Energy Monterey Energy Group
Contractor Groza Construction and Tom Duteau
Sprayed Earth Contractor Delta Gunite Solano Inc.

Lake Tahoe Retreat
Architect Turnbull Griffin Haesloop
Interiors Jonathan Straley Designs
Structural MKM & Associates
Contractor M & R Construction

Sebastopol Camp
Architect Turnbull Griffin Haesloop
Landscape Architect Landscape Office LTD
Interiors John and Loreta Hornall
Structural Fratessa Forbes Wong
Energy BEC Associates
Contractor Sawyer Construction

Grace Magill Arts and Science Building, Burke's School
Architect Turnbull Griffin Haesloop
Landscape Architect GLS
Structural Fratessa Forbes Wong
Mechanical Guttmann & Blaevoet
Electrical, Lighting O'Mahoney & Myer
Acoustical Walsh-Norris Associates
Graphic Design Kim Urbain
Contractor Plant Construction

Atherton Retreat
Architect Turnbull Griffin Haesloop
Landscape Architect Lutsko Associates
Interiors Turnbull Griffin Haesloop
Structural Fratessa Forbes Wong
Energy BEC Associates
Lighting Eric Johnson Lighting Design
Contractor Carter Seddon Construction

Sea Ranch Meadow I
Architect Turnbull Griffin Haesloop
Landscape Architect Joni L. Janecki & Associates
Interiors Robert Stein / Turnbull Griffin Haesloop
Structural Jon Brody Consulting Engineers
Energy BEC Associates
Contractor Don Matheny Construction

Sea Ranch Meadow II
Architect Turnbull Griffin Haesloop
Landscape Architect Joni L. Janecki & Associates
Interiors Robert Stein / Turnbull Griffin Haesloop
Structural Fratessa Forbes Wong
Energy Energy Calc Co
Lighting EJA Lighting Design
Contractor Empire Contracting Inc. with Eric Jackson

The Commons, Branson School
Architect Turnbull Griffin Haesloop
Landscape Architect Landscape Office Ltd.
Structural Fratessa Forbes Wong
Energy, LEED Loisos + Ubbelohde
Mechanical Lefler Engineering
Electrical, Lighting O'Mahoney & Myer
Food Service Presidio Design Group
Acoustical Walsh-Norris Associates
Civil Sherwood Design
Contractor Herrero Construction

Douglas Fine Arts Center, Branson School
Architect Turnbull Griffin Haesloop
Landscape Architect Landscape Office Ltd.
Structural Fratessa Forbes Wong
Energy, LEED Loisos + Ubbelohde
Mechanical Lefler Engineering
Electrical, Lighting O'Mahoney & Myer
Acoustical Walsh-Norris Associates
Civil Sherwood Design
Contractor Herrero Construction

Hicks Mountain Ranch
Architect Turnbull Griffin Haesloop
Landscape Architect SWA Group
Interiors Lotus Bleu Design
Structural Fratessa Forbes Wong
Energy Loisos + Ubbelohde
Civil Sherwood Design
Contractor Redhorse Constructors

Marin Hillside
Architect Turnbull Griffin Haesloop
Landscape Architect GLS
Interiors Turnbull Griffin Haesloop
Structural Fratessa Forbes Wong
Energy Stantec
Civil Sherwood Design
Contractor Redhorse Constructors

College Track San Francisco
Architect Turnbull Griffin Haesloop
Historic Resources Page & Turnbull
Interiors Turnbull Griffin Haesloop
Structural Fratessa Forbes Wong
Energy Loisos + Ubbelohde
Mechanical, Electrical Randall Lamb
Project Manager Michael Simmons Property Management
Contractor Plant Construction

Sausalito Hillside Remodel
Architect Turnbull Griffin Haesloop
Landscape Architect Scott Lewis Landscape Architecture
Interiors Turnbull Griffin Haesloop
Structural Fratessa Forbes Wong
Energy Energy Calc Co
Civil ILS Associates
Contractor Redhorse Constructors, Jeff King and Co

Coyote Camp
Architect Turnbull Griffin Haesloop
Landscape Architect DELA
Interiors Turnbull Griffin Haesloop
Structural Fratessa Forbes Wong
Contractor Kent Drescher, Builder

Hupomone Ranch
Architect Turnbull Griffin Haesloop
Landscape Architect Lutsko Assocoates
Interiors Erin Martin Design
Structural MKM & Associates
Mechanical, Geothermal Meline Engineering
Energy Loisos + Ubbelohde
LEED Michael Heacock + Associates
Contractor Sawyer Construction

Cloverdale Vineyard
Architect Turnbull Griffin Haesloop
Landscape Architect DELA
Structural MKM & Associates
Energy Energy Calc Co
Civil Kelder Engineering
Contractor Kennedy Construction

Berkeley Cottage
Architect Turnbull Griffin Haesloop
Landscape Architect Site Studio Landscape Architecture
Interiors Turnbull Griffin Haesloop
Structural Fratessa Forbes Wong
Energy Loisos + Ubbelohde
Contractor Sawyer Construction

Sonoma Retreat
Architect Turnbull Griffin Haesloop
Landscape Architect SWA Group
Interiors Turnbull Griffin Haesloop
Structural Fratessa Forbes Wong
Energy Loisos + Ubbelohde
Mechanical Meline Engineering
Civil Adobe Associates
Contractor JMA

Stinson Beach Lagoon
Architect Turnbull Griffin Haesloop
Landscape Architect Las Baulinas Nursery
Interiors Cleaveland & Kennedy Design
Structural Fratessa Forbes Wong
Energy Energy Calc Co
Contractor Sawyer Construction

Portola Valley Garden
Architect Turnbull Griffin Haesloop
Landscape Architect Scott Lewis Landscape Architecture
Interiors Turnbull Griffin Haesloop
Structural Fratessa Forbes Wong
Energy Loisos + Ubbelohde
Mechanical Meline Engineering
Water Harvesting Watersprout
Civil BKF
Contractor Pete Moffat Construction

Skyfall, The Sea Ranch
Architect Turnbull Griffin Haesloop
Interior Stylist Cleaveland & Kennedy Design
Structural I.L. Welty & Associates
Energy Energy Calc Co
Contractor Empire Contracting Inc.

Carmel Valley Retreat
Architect Turnbull Griffin Haesloop
Landscape Architect Ground Studio
Interiors Jorie Clark Design
Structural Fratessa Forbes Wong
Energy Loisos + Ubbelohde
Mechanical Meline Engineering
Lighting EJA Lighting Design
Civil Whitson Engineers
Contractor Vucina Construction
Sprayed Earth Contractor Delta Gunnite Solano Inc.

Healdsburg Knoll
Architect Turnbull Griffin Haesloop
Landscape Architect ReedGilliland Landscape Architects
Interiors Studio Collins Weir
Structural Jon Brody Consulting Engineers
Energy Loisos + Ubbelohde
Mechanical Meline Engineering
Acoustical Walsh-Norris Associates
Civil Munselle Civil Engineers
Contractor Fairweather & Associates

Acknowledgments

Jan Hartman has been the guiding force behind the creation of this book. She developed the schedules, edited the text and essays, oversaw our contributors, and eventually offered the proposal for the monograph to Rizzoli USA. She has continued to be our sage editor as we have worked with Rizzoli on all the decisions and details of bringing this book to publication. She has been a delight to work with and has championed our work and our book. We are deeply grateful to Jan.

Another of Jan's key contributions was to suggest the talented Benjamin English to design the book. Ben has been attentive, flexible, and creative. His design is beautiful. He has also patiently incorporated our many comments and modifications. We are so grateful to Ben.

Eric and I acknowledge and honor our esteemed contributors for their insightful essays: Paul Goldberger, Daniel Gregory, and Donlyn Lyndon. Each piece is filled with fascinating observations reflecting their lens on the work of Turnbull Griffin Haesloop.

We thank our generous clients who allowed us to include their projects in the monograph. We honor the photographers who documented our buildings with such clarity and precision and acknowledge them for allowing us to use their photographs.

We acknowledge the hard work, talent, and friendship of the architects and designers from within Turnbull Griffin Haesloop and the many consultants and contractors we collaborated with to create these buildings. It was a team effort.

Waverly Lowell accepted the archives of Turnbull Griffin Haesloop into the Environmental Design Archives at UC Berkeley, which prompted us to undertake this book. Thank you, Waverly.

We thank our friends and mentors for their advice and encouragement on the book project including Kenny Caldwell, Gordon Goff, Marianne Haesloop, Laura Hartman, Stefan Hastrup, Pierluigi Serraino, Robert Stein, William Stout, Connor Turnbull, Margaret Turnbull, and David Wakely. A special thanks to Matt Au and Yan Huang for helping prepare the drawings.

Finally, we extend our thanks to Rizzoli International Publications for all the careful attention to publishing our book, especially the efforts of Charles Miers, Douglas Curran, and Alexia Casaús Leppo.

Contributors

Paul Goldberger, whom *The Huffington Post* has called "the leading figure in architecture criticism," began his career at *The New York Times*, where in 1984 he was awarded the Pulitzer Prize for Distinguished Criticism, the highest award in journalism. From 1997 to 2011 he served as the Architecture Critic for *The New Yorker* and is now a Contributing Editor at *Vanity Fair*. He is the author of numerous books, including *BALLPARK: Baseball in the American City* and *Building Art: The Life and Work of Frank Gehry* (Alfred A. Knopf); *Building with History* (Prestel); *Why Architecture Matters* (Yale University Press); *Building Up and Tearing Down* (Monacelli); and *Christo and Jeanne-Claude* (Taschen). His latest books include *Blue Dream and the Legacy of Modernism in the Hamptons* (Delmonico Books, 2023) and *DUMBO: The Making of a Neighborhood and the Rebirth of Brooklyn* (Rizzoli, 2021). He holds the Joseph Urban Chair in Design and Architecture at The New School in New York City and was formerly Dean of the Parsons School of Design at The New School. The Vincent Scully Prize from the National Building Museum in 2012 recognized the influence of his writing on the public's understanding of architecture. In 2017 he received the Award in Architecture of the American Academy of Arts and Letters, which called him "the doyen of American architectural critics." He was named a Literary Lion by the New York Public Library in 1993, and the New York Landmarks Conservancy named him one of its "Living Landmarks" in 2023. He is chairman of the Advisory Council of The Glass House, a property of the National Trust for Historic Preservation, and is also a member of the Boards of Trustees of the Gund Gallery at Kenyon College, the Urban Design Forum, and the New York Stem Cell Foundation, and he is an emeritus trustee of the National Trust for Historic Preservation and Kenyon College.

Daniel P. Gregory is a graduate of Yale University with a PhD in architectural history from the University of California at Berkeley. He grew up in Northern California, in a house designed by William Wurster. He served as senior home editor of *Sunset* magazine and editor in chief of Houseplans.com, and is the author of *Cliff May and the Modern Ranch House* (Rizzoli, 2008); *From the Land: The Architecture of Backen Gillam & Kroeger* (Rizzoli, 2012); and *The Farm: Contemporary Rural Architecture* (Princeton Architectural Press, 2020), as well as numerous essays about Bay Area architecture.

Donlyn Lyndon was a partner of Moore, Lyndon, Turnbull, and Whitaker (MLTW), architects for the award-winning Condominium One at The Sea Ranch in Sonoma County, California—now on the National Register of Historic Places. Lyndon was chair of the schools of architecture at the University of Oregon, MIT, and the University of California, Berkeley, where he is Professor Emeritus of Architecture and Urban Design. He served as president of the Association of Collegiate Schools of Architecture (ACSA) and received the American Institute of Architects and ACSA's Topaz Medallion for outstanding contributions in architectural education. He is author or coauthor of *The Place of Houses*; *Chambers for a Memory Palace*; *The Sea Ranch: Fifty Years of Architecture, Landscape, Place, and Community on the Northern California Coast*; and *Place at The Sea Ranch: Landscape/Architecture Markers on our Trails*. He founded the journal *PLACES* and is now a resident at The Sea Ranch.

Photography

Jim Alinder 58 bottom, 114, 115 third from top, 116

Marion Brenner 37

Mark Darley ©1994 292 top and middle

Joe Fletcher 4, 73, 74, 76–81, 82

Mary Griffin 292 bottom

Eric Haesloop 24, 25, 112, 113, 152, 194, 216 bottom left, 265 bottom

Proctor Jones 19 bottom, 26, 27

Courtesy of the Jones Family 22

Matthew Millman 19 second from top, 23, 28, 29, 30, 61–69, 70, 179–81, 182, 184, 185, 186, 205, 206, 208–13, 219–21, 222, 224–27

Adam Rouse 282, 285

Cesar Rubio 294 top and bottom

SA Sanderson 164

Shaun Sullivan 234 bottom, 236, 237 bottom

Environmental Design Archives, UC Berkeley 19 third from top

David Wakely cover, 2, 10, 11, 14, 16–18, 19 top, 20, 21, 33, 34, 35, 36, 38, 39, 41–49, 51, 52, 55, 56, 58 top, 85–93, 95–97, 99, 100, 102, 104, 105, 106, 108–11, 115 top and middle, 117, 119–23, 125–33, 134, 137, 139–41, 142, 144, 145, 147, 148, 150, 151, 153–59, 160, 163, 165, 166, 168, 169, 170, 172, 173, 175–77, 189–91, 192, 195, 196, 198–203, 215–17, 229–31, 232, 234 top, 235, 239, 240 242–53, 255–57, 258, 260–64, 265 top, 267–69, 270, 272–77, 279–81, 284, 286, 288–89, 290, 303

To the memory of William Turnbull Jr.

First published in the United States of America
in 2025 by
Rizzoli International Publications, Inc.
49 West 27th Street
New York, NY 10001
www.rizzoliusa.com

Copyright © 2025 Turnbull Griffin Haesloop
Foreword: Paul Goldberger
Texts: Mary Griffin, Eric Haesloop,
Daniel P. Gregory, Donlyn Lyndon, and
Margaret Turnbull

All rights reserved. No part of this publication
may be reproduced, stored in a retrieval
system, or transmitted in any form or by any
means, electronic, mechanical, photocopying,
recording, or otherwise, without prior consent
of the publishers.

Publisher: Charles Miers
Edited by Douglas Curran and Alexia Casaús Leppo
Produced by Jan Hartman
Designed by Benjamin English
Production Manager: Barbara Sadick
Managing Editor: Lynn Scrabis

ISBN: 978-0-8478-7577-1
Library of Congress Control Number: 2025905594

Printed in China
2025 2026 2027 2028 / 10 9 8 7 6 5 4 3 2 1

The authorized representative in the EU for
product safety and compliance is
Mondadori Libri S.p.A., via Gian Battista Vico 42,
Milan, Italy, 20123, www.mondadori.it

Visit us online:
Instagram.com/RizzoliBooks
Facebook.com/RizzoliNewYork
X: @Rizzoli_Books
Youtube.com/user/RizzoliNY